DAVID GRAHAM
FROM RIDICULE TO ACCLAIM

by

RUSSELL JAMES

RYAN PUBLISHING

First published 2012 in Australia by Ryan Publishing
PO Box 7680, Melbourne, 3004
Victoria, Australia
Ph: 61 3 9505 6820 Fax: 61 3 9505 6821
Email: books@ryanpub.com
Website: www.ryanpub.com

National Library of Australia Cataloguing-in-Publication entry

Author: James, Russell, 1942-

Title: David Graham : from ridicule to acclaim / by Russell James
Edited by Graeme Ryan.

ISBN: 9781876498641 (pbk.)
ISBN: 9781876498706 (ebook: epub)
Notes: Includes index.

Subjects: Graham, David, 1946-
    US PGA Championship
    US Open Golf Championship
    Australian Open Golf ChampionshipGolfers—Australia—Biography
    Golf—Tournaments—United States
    Golf—Tournaments—Australia

Dewey Number: 796.352092

Copyright © Russell James

Apart from any fair dealing for the purposes of private study, research, criticism or review, as permitted under the Copyright Act, no part may be reproduced by any process without written permission. Inquiries should be addressed to the publishers.

Cover and internal design by Luke Harris, Chameleon Design, Victoria, Australia.

CONTENTS

PREFACE "What a high price I paid." v

THE DAVID GRAHAM FILE 1

CHAPTER

1. "My love of golf was only exceeded by my hatred of school." 5
2. "I worked like a slave, but couldn't have had a better boss." 13
3. "You're digging a hole for yourself here, come with me to Sydney." . 21
4. "The officials wanted me to give the trophy back." 27
5. "I thought I was a big shot. Really, I didn't know the first thing about the game." 35
6. "Learning to play golf instead of golf playing me." 43
7. "I'll win it for you one day, boss." 51
8. "At the apex of his career he was about as convivial as a Trappist monk." 59
9. "Anybody can get lucky and win a major championship once. It takes a great player to win two." 71
10. "Making hay while the sun shines." 81
11. "The Seniors Tour was my saving grace." 93
12. "I cried. I cried absolutely. So did my wife." 99
13. "It was the end of me as a golfer. It was almost the end of me, full stop." 109
14. "How do you put Isao Aoki in before David Graham?" 115

CONTENTS

APPENDIX

I   Eight letters written by David Graham to George Naismith from 20 March 1968 to 24 August 1979 119

II   Article from *The Evening Independent* of Florida, 7 December 1973 128

III   Report by Peter Stone in the *Sydney Morning Herald* 1 August 1976 129

INDEX 131

PREFACE   "What a high price I paid."

David Graham, one of Australia's best ever golfers, "is abrasive and dogmatically opinionated. He can convey an impression of arrogance which is not entirely without substance." These words appeared in the London newspaper, *The Observer*, the day after David Graham won the 1981 US Open Golf Championship. Their author was the noted golf writer Peter Dobereiner. Another respected golf correspondent, Peter Allis, described the young Australian in even less flattering terms. "He is a rather hard and sometimes bitter man", he wrote soon after the Australian's greatest triumph.

Descriptions such as these are not uncommon. From his very early days as a 14-year old trainee professional at Melbourne's Riversdale Golf Club, Anthony David Graham frequently rubbed many people 'up the wrong way'. Certainly very few of his fellow trainees had a good word to say about him. As a 17-year old trainee graduate starting out in the 'hit or miss' world of Monday pro-am events and later, on the Australian secondary tournament circuit, he quickly gained a reputation as being bad tempered, sullen and morose with little or no sense of humour.

When, in the early 1970s, he began to have some successes on Australia's main PGA Tour and in Asia, he did precious little to befriend himself with other golfers. Also, tournament officials, sponsors, caddies, galleries and hotel staff often felt the brunt of his volatile temper. Significantly, David Graham's anger with the world even extended to himself, and in no small measure.

By his own admission David Graham was "a brooder and a loner." "I possessed a fierce temper and was scared to death of showing any emotion to anyone", he said. David Graham was the epitome of 'the angry young man'. When he played competitive golf it was always in a painfully slow manner and with little regard for his playing partners or any spectators. Probably the most damning criticism levelled at him was from some of his fellow professionals, "who dreaded being paired with him for a tournament round."

Despite the many condemnations of him there were a few observers who thought it might just be a case of David Graham being extremely difficult to get to know. In this respect Peter Allis likened him to the great Ben Hogan. "Both men," he noted, "had desperate struggles in their early days and both were very cautious in forming friendships." In the immediate aftermath of Graham's US Open victory in 1981, Allis recalled that Hogan and Jack Nicklaus were, in the early stages of their careers, respected for their golf games but not really admired for their temperaments, on and even off, the golf course. "The world learned to love Hogan and Nicklaus as well as respect them," he concluded, "perhaps the same sort of thing will happen to the new US Open Champion."

Put simply this didn't happen. David Graham never achieved the widespread admiration that was afforded Hogan and Nicklaus nor that which many other major winners achieved in their careers. His reputation as the 'hard man' of world golf followed him throughout his playing days. But the David Graham of more recent years has mellowed, is less confrontational and certainly more personable.

This is not to say that David Graham no longer speaks his mind or frequently offends some people as a consequence. *Golf Digest* magazine, when interviewing him several years ago, described him as "a hard-edged character, irredeemingly stubborn, blunt and dogmatic." This is probably an accurate description of the man today but one that needs to be tempered by the views of some of his peers. Fellow Australian golfer, Bruce Devlin, sees Graham as "honest, yes, even brutally honest, yet fiercely protective of his family and unswervingly loyal to his closest friends."

Even David Graham's severest critics acknowledge that his approach to golf, and life, has been influenced by the desperate struggles of his early days. A truant from school as a young boy, getting into fights that he never won, ridiculed as a loner, branded a loser, ostracised by his father at age fourteen, much of it was, in Graham's own words, "pure hell." Yet somehow he succeeded in spite of his upbringing and, it must be said, in spite of himself.

The years of "pain, discouragement and torment" helped make David Graham the type of golfer he became. That is, hard-edged, dour, resolute and always fiercely competitive. He practised longer than anyone else. He studied the technical aspects of the golf swing with religious fervour. He spent many hours willing himself to be mentally tough. Right from the outset he developed a thick outer shell to withstand the barbs and put-downs that continually came his way.

David Graham gave his whole life to golf but, as the man himself now reflects, "What a high price I paid."

David Graham through the hitting zone with perfect balance, timing and power.

THE DAVID GRAHAM FILE

- Born May 23, 1946 in St Kilda, Victoria, Australia.
- Turned professional in 1962.

Victories:

37 worldwide.

Two time major winner:
1979 US PGA Championship
1981 US Open Championship

6 other wins on US PGA Tour:
1972 Cleveland Open
1976 Westchester Classic
1976 American Golf Classic
1980 Memorial Tournament
1981 Phoenix Open
1983 Houston Open

6 wins on Australian PGA Tour:
1970 Tasmanian Open
1970 Victorian Open
1975 Wills Masters Tournament
1977 Australian Open Championship
1979 West Lakes Classic
1985 Queensland Open

14 International wins:
1970 Thailand Open
1970 French Open
1971 Caracas Open (Venuzeula)
1971 JAL Open (Japan)
1976 Chunichi Crowns Invitational (Japan)
1976 World Match Play Championship
1977 South African Open
1978 Mexico Cup
1979 New Zealand Open
1980 Mexican Open
1980 Rolex Tournament (Japan)
1980 Brazil Classic
1981 Lancome Trophy (France)
1982 Lancome Trophy (France)

5 wins on the US Senior Tour:
1997 GTE Classic
1997 South West Bell Dominion Tournament
1997 Comfort Classic
1998 Royal Caribbean Classic
1999 Raleys Gold Rush Classic

3 Team wins: (representing Australia)
1970 World Cup (with Bruce Devlin)
1985 Dunhill Cup (with Greg Norman and Graham Marsh)
1986 Dunhill Cup (with Greg Norman and Rodger Davis)

Also:
1994 Australian Skins

12 times in top 10 at a Major Championship (excluding 2 wins):

1976	US PGA	–	tied 4th
1977	The Masters	–	tied 6th
1978	The Masters	–	tied 9th
1979	US Open	–	tied 7th
1980	The Masters	–	5th
1981	The Masters	–	7th
1982	US Open	–	tied 6th
1983	US Open	–	tied 8th
1984	The Masters	–	tied 6th
1985	The Masters	–	tied 10th
1985	British Open	–	tied 3rd
1986	US PGA	–	tied 7th

1

"MY LOVE OF GOLF WAS ONLY EXCEEDED BY MY HATRED OF SCHOOL"

For the slightly built twelve-year old, the bicycle ride from school to his home put him 'somewhere between a rock and a hard place'. School provided few, if any, rewarding experiences for David. Home was far from being a happy one. There, in the small weatherboard house, his parents fought often and loudly. Years later, when looking back at those turbulent years, his mother, Patricia, surmised that "it was perhaps no-one's fault and yet it was everyone's fault. At that time only bitterness and anger seemed to exist."

It was on one of these bike rides home from school that the young David Graham saw something that was to become his respite, indeed his escape, from the travails of home and school. Passing by an open field he noticed a solitary figure hitting golf balls from one side of the field to the other. Getting off his bike he stood and watched, with growing interest, the man's intense concentration over each ball before unleashing a powerful, fluent swing. David was particularly taken by the flight of the balls as they left the face of the golf club and arced in the overcast sky to land softly on the green turf some distance away. These images remained with him as he eventually continued his journey home.

Putting his bicycle in the garage he quickly set about to find some implements with which he could attempt to imitate what he had just seen. All he could find was a hockey stick and an old tennis ball. Undeterred he started playing golf, of sorts, in the backyard of the Burwood house.

For several days his after school pursuit of that 'little white tennis ball' with the somewhat battered hockey stick continued unabated. When his mother realised it was golf, not hockey, that was his new found interest she recalled that some years previously she too had dabbled, albeit briefly, with the royal and ancient game. More importantly, she had bought a few second-hand clubs that were now "somewhere amongst the accumulated mess of the garage." It didn't take long for David Graham to find them. They were gathering dust behind a stack of empty boxes and, as a bonus, were all sitting in a narrow little canvas golf bag.

Perhaps fate had willed that the little canvas bag and its handful of golf clubs were just waiting for the right young boy to find them. That young boy was definitely David Graham. In real need of some diversion from his unhappy life they appeared at exactly the right time and place.

But there was one problem. David was a natural right-hander in everything he did yet his mother's clubs were left-handed. This proved to be only a temporary setback. David Graham would become a left-handed golfer and, with the couple of discoloured balls that were found in the side pocket of the bag, immediately began "knocking the ball around south-paw fashion on an oval near the house."

From the day he discovered those clubs in the garage, David did little else in his spare time except hit golf balls. His mother remembered one early evening in particular. "He rushed in just as I was preparing tea and implored me to 'come and have a look'. 'I can now hit it from one lot of goal posts through the ones up at the other end of the oval. Come on, come and see for yourself!' So urgent was his plea that I, as it turned out, left the chops to burn and the potatoes to boil dry, and followed him out to the oval. Sure enough, he would line up a golf ball and with an almighty swipe send the ball, split cover and all, on its way. I must admit it was exciting."

The after school and weekend golf continued but with an emerging earnestness that before long was to materialise into an obsession. As he was to say later "my love of golf was now only exceeded by my hatred of school." By the time he turned thirteen, David had 'outgrown' the local oval and was hitting golf balls at a local nine-hole golf course, Wattle Park. He was now skipping school on a regular basis. On these days he would get dressed in the morning and pretend to go off to school but never actually get there. Instead he would ride his bicycle to Wattle Park and "hang around the golf shop and go hit balls on the driving range." "It certainly beat school," he said in 1990, "where I was far from being a good student. I had few friends and got into a lot of fights, none of which I won due to my small size."

* * *

Chapter 1

Soon after his thirteenth birthday, David Graham joined the Wattle Park Golf Club as a junior member. Bob Patey, a long time Wattle Park member, has this memory of David Graham. "He was a desperately keen thirteen-year old left-hander, striving to make the C grade pennant team. Unfortunately he couldn't make the team, he was so slightly built and had a very big slice, but it certainly wasn't for want of trying."

David's efforts were however not without their reward. He played in, and won, the club's junior championship. He was presented with a tiny little cup. It was his very first trophy and, regardless of what was to come his way in later years, remained a most prized possession throughout his golfing career.

Local teenager, Neil Hudson, was his opponent in the final and recalls, "After I missed a two foot (60cm) putt at the eighteenth to lose the match, David ran around the perimeter of the green like a circus pony, whooping with delight and punching the air in triumph."

A few weeks after his first championship victory, Patricia Graham noticed that her son had become much quieter than usual. He was, she acknowledged, "a bit more headstrong than most boys of his age and never able to stay still or relax." She thought his subdued mood meant that something had gone wrong at school. "But no!" she would write later, "suddenly he burst forth. It was as if he had been bottling something up inside for some time and now he wanted it out."

And out it all came! "You are not going to like this, I know, but I have decided what I want to be. I am going to be the best golfer in the world. Don't try and change my mind. I'm sorry but just you wait and see, I'll show you." That exclamation was typical of a young David Graham. Right from the outset his attitude was not, 'I want to be', or, 'I would like to be', but straight onto the front foot with, "I am going to be." It was an attitude that would fuel his drive to succeed at golf, yet also one that would frequently put him 'offside' with other golfers and golf officials.

Patricia's reaction to her son's outburst was, in turn, typical of most mothers when faced with such a heartfelt pronouncement. "Initially", she reflected, "I was full of anxiety for it is common knowledge that many dream of stardom only to fall by the wayside, reduced to floundering forever in and out of jobs. I decided to show as little reaction to his announcement as possible and see what the passing of some time would bring to his grandiose plans. But as the months went by I sensed that his determination to be a golfer only got stronger."

These months came at a crucial stage in David Graham's life. With his desire to make golf his chosen career, and a father who continued to make things difficult for everyone in the Graham home, he was very fortunate to have two professional golfers, both very experienced and highly respected, put him on a pathway which would turn his dream into reality. The first was John Crean, the professional at Wattle Park. The other was the long serving professional at Riversdale Golf Club, George Naismith.

John Crean was intrigued by David's total dedication to practice. He devoted numerous hours advising and coaching the young lad, many of which, in truth, David should have been spending at school. He also had the wisdom to perceive that schoolwork was most definitely not David's forte, a career as a golf professional just possibly might be.

* * *

As David approached his fourteenth birthday his determination to leave school grew stronger. Well aware of David's passion for golf, at the exclusion of virtually everything else, it was Crean who, according to Patricia Graham, "came up with the suggestion that was to change his life forever. He told David that if he wanted to be a professional golfer the road ahead would be a hard one but the best man for him to serve his traineeship under was George Naismith." Patricia Graham added, "within an hour David was at the Riversdale pro-shop pleading his case."

George Naismith, like John Crean, saw something very different in the skinny, rather dishevelled young teenager that stood before him. He had not considered taking on another apprentice. However, at the boy's urgings, George agreed to give him a trial period in the pro-shop, working during the upcoming May school holidays.

David Graham worked long and hard during those holidays in a variety of somewhat menial tasks, none of which involved him actually hitting a golf ball. David's enthusiasm for golf at the expense of continuing his schooling was being deliberately tested by Naismith. Nearly four decades earlier, George had also made a decision to leave school on his fourteenth birthday and take up a traineeship at Melbourne's famous Kingston Heath Golf Club under the supervision of professional, Ernie Woods. That decision to leave Brighton Technical School where George, unlike David Graham, was a popular and capable student, was uniformly criticised by his family and teachers. Naismith did make a success of a playing and club professional career, but knew full well that many trainee graduates had struggled to survive and had left golf usually to find that their lack of schooling severely limited their employment prospects.

The last day of the school holidays, arrived. George hadn't told David what his decision would be. Both he and his mother were apprehensive to say the least. In her own words she describes that fateful day. "I was sent for. Was there to be any future for David at Riversdale? Relief, there was! David was to start his apprenticeship with George a few days later, on his fourteenth birthday. I distinctly recall two comments made that day. The first was to David by George. Well aware of David's fierce desire to be a tournament player he cautioned him, 'You might make it son, you might not. We'll just have to wait and see'. The second was, as we walked home, from a boy as happy and excited as I had ever seen him. 'Mum', he said looking up at me, 'it is the best birthday present I could ever have wished for'."

Back in the Burwood home, someone else had a very different view of the day's events. George Graham was firmly against his son's decision to leave school. A stern man, hardened by his wartime experiences in the navy, he told David that he would "kick him out of the house" if he followed through with his intention to become a trainee professional.

* * *

In a 1990 interview, David Graham described what happened when his father first heard of what he intended to do. "My father never did take kindly to being defied. When I told him I was quitting school to work at Riversdale, all hell broke loose. However thanks to my mother's intervention he didn't kick me out despite his initial threats to do so. I was allowed to stay in the house although I was quartered in the back part of it along with my mother. My father and my older sister lived in the front part of the house and for the next year or so, until David and his mother moved out to another house, I hardly ever saw them."

George Graham was much truer to his word in one other respect. He had vowed not to speak to his son "ever again" and, from that day up to his death in 2007, he 'broke his silence' on just the one occasion. That occasion was the 1970 US Open Championship, held that year at Hazeltine Golf Club in the state of Minnesota.

David Graham had left Australia to live in the USA in 1969 and the 1970 US Open was to be the first time he would tee it up in one of golf's four major championships. On one of the days leading up to the start of the US Open he was practising diligently on the practice range when a course marshal approached him. The marshal told David that there was a gentleman in the gallery who would like to talk to him. When David asked "Who is it?" the marshal replied, "He says he is your father."

David stopped practising and walked over to the ropes. To his considerable surprise it was indeed his father standing there. George Graham indicated that he would like to buy his son lunch. Somewhat hesitantly David agreed and the two of them retired to the clubhouse. There, George Graham began to apologise to his son for their past 'history'. He tried to give his side of the story but David was unimpressed. "I didn't feel he was all that sincere, and what he said to me included a lot of things which were really not appropriate." He summed up their brief conversation. "I really didn't want to hear any of it and I told him so, and that was it."

David Graham never saw or talked to his father again. Years later, after the death of his father, he reiterated his feelings of that June day in 1970. "He was like a complete stranger to me. He had fought in the Second World War. People like that had to be tough to survive, so I try to understand. Am I sorry I never patched things up before he passed away? No, I am not. It was his choice to try and do so at Hazeltine, not mine. I was more concerned with my career and my marriage."

David Graham's relationship with his father contrasted sharply with the one he had with his mother, Patricia. Yet the closeness of mother and son, so important to David in his early years, was also not to last. According to Graham, he and his wife Maureen, kept in touch with her for some considerable time after he moved to America, but he admitted that, some twenty odd years later, contact with her had been lost. Speaking briefly about it several years ago he said "She had a number of relationships after separating from my father that, I believe, weren't very good also, and eventually she became reclusive."

To what extent Patricia Graham became reclusive in her later years is difficult to assess. It remains a sad, but perhaps significant fact, that David Graham lost or severed contact with his father and sister during his mid-teen years and his devoted mother some time after he went to live in America.

2.

"I WORKED LIKE A SLAVE, BUT COULDN'T HAVE HAD A BETTER BOSS"

Three decades later David Graham had clear memories of his first week at Riversdale Golf Club. "The first person who ever significantly impacted on my life, bless his heart, was the professional at Riversdale, George Naismith. He was just a wonderful gentleman. He won the Australian Open in 1937. Peter Thomson also did his apprenticeship under Mr Naismith."

"At the start of the May school holidays, and a week short of my fourteenth birthday, I went over there and he gave me a job for the rest of the school holidays, a trial run, as it were. I showed up the next morning and he told me "You have to go home, young fellow, and put on a tie." He was very old school. My first day on the job, he started me taking apart rusty pull-carts and sanding the paint off them. There were about 70 of them and it took me forever."

In 1948, when Peter Thomson decided to turn professional, he had to serve, like everyone else, a three-year apprenticeship with an accredited PGA professional. Australia's leading golfer at the time, Norman Von Nida, strongly advised Thomson to start his training with George Naismith at Riversdale Golf Club. It didn't take long for Thomson to be deeply impressed by Naismith's methods and thoughtful manner. "George Naismith was as big an influence on my career as anybody," he says. "He was a most generous and likeable man who always had a smile on his face." There can be no underestimating Naismith's contribution to Thomson's career. He helped shape the lad's future by allowing him to compete overseas whilst still an assistant. Many claimed Naismith gave Thomson too much latitude but Naismith was a shrewd judge and realised his assistant was unique.

George Naismith is chaired by fellow competitors after winning the 1937 Australian Open at The Australian GC in Sydney. Photo published in The Argus.

Chapter 2

Several years later when another gifted youngster came to work for him, he reacted in the same supportive and encouraging manner. David Graham said of George, "He was one of the very, very special people of this world. I spent about four years with him and one of his strong points was that he was able to detect skill in a young player and, more importantly, teach that player manners and how to grow up right. Peter and I were both very fortunate to have a deep association with him in the early stages of our careers. We couldn't have had a better boss." "There (at Riversdale) I worked like a slave, taking only one day off every two weeks. I often worked twelve hours a day, doing every odd job you can think of. My salary was eight pounds (AU$16) a week."

David devoted every free moment he had to practising. Between the ages of fifteen and seventeen, when he wasn't working around the club, he was out on the range hitting balls. "I would hit them and pick them up, hit them and pick them up, until it was too dark to see. "Sometimes", he reflected, "I would sleep on the sofa in the pro-shop instead of going home."

Because his home environment wasn't very happy, Riversdale became David Graham's refuge. "It was a nice club," he said in 1988. "I had to wear a collar and tie and be on my best behaviour at all times. I was young and, socially, quite green. On occasions I would call a member by his wrong name and get in trouble for it, but Mr Naismith was always there to bail me out. There is no question, that if it weren't for his help, I would have become a juvenile delinquent. I had no friends my own age and, hence, none of the companionship that is so important to young teenagers."

* * *

David played left-handed in those early days at Riversdale, unbeknown to George Naismith. But twelve months or so into his traineeship this was all about to change. He explained his switch thus. "Mr Naismith didn't know I was playing left-handed because as trainees we weren't even allowed out on the golf course until late at night. After I had been working there for about a year he stopped his car on the way home beside the driving range. He got out of his car and watched me hit a couple of 2-wood shots. They went all right but he asked me what was my strongest hand. I told him it was my right hand. It was explained to me that the strongest hand needs to be on the bottom of the club not on the top as it was with my left-handed grip. It was that night on the practice tee that Mr Naismith told me that I must change to playing right-handed. "Go build yourself some right-handed clubs in the shop," he told me, "practise with them and I will check you again in six months." "He then scratched an arc in the patchy grass on the practice tee. It was to indicate the plane of the take-away, and the follow-through after impact, of my 'new' right-handed swing. I didn't argue, after all he was the boss! I just said OK. As I slowly learned to play right-handed I practised even harder. I didn't play a competitive round for nearly a year and it was at least eighteen months before I won anything competing against the other assistants and playing right-handed."

Although he switched from left to right-handed, David Graham still preferred to putt left-handed. One evening when it got too dark to hit balls on the practice fairway, he went to the practice putting green in front of the clubhouse. He had been there only a few minutes when George came over to him from the adjacent pro-shop. David thought Naismith had already left to drive home. Actually George had forgotten something and had returned to get it. Naismith was not impressed with David's left-handed putting and told him in no uncertain terms that David was to do everything on the golf course right-handed.

This message, it would seem, needed to be repeated before it sank in. John Montague lived near David Graham and had been a junior member with David at Wattle Park. John also went to Riversdale, as a junior member, a year or so after David started his apprenticeship there. The two boys would often practise their putting together late in the afternoon on the practice green in front of the clubhouse. John recalls one such session being suddenly interrupted by the loud cry of 'here David catch this'. David barely had time to reach out with his hand and grab the golf club that George had tossed in his direction. He did catch the club and with his right hand. Pointing to it, George reminded his young apprentice, "That's why I told you to do everything on the golf course right-handed, and that includes putting!"

* * *

Chapter 2

Three well known Melbourne identities also have distinct memories of a young David Graham 'serving his time' at Riversdale Golf Club.

Bill Barrot, the brilliant centreman for Richmond (Australian Rules) Football Club was, as a youth, a caddy at Riversdale. He was also keen to leave school to get a job and had his eyes on an apprenticeship under George Naismith. Somewhat annoyed at missing out on the job and, soon after, at David Graham's insistence that Barrot couldn't use the practice fairway until after four o'clock in the afternoon, young Bill 'dropped' Graham with a straight left through an open side window of the pro-shop. The great irony of Graham getting the apprenticeship over Barrot is that Naismith was a fanatical one-eyed supporter of the Richmond Tigers. Little did George know then that David Graham would go on to win two majors while 'bustling Billy Barrot' would help his beloved Tigers win two premierships and represent Victoria eleven times during an illustrious football career.

Lindsay Gitsham, a trainee in the same year as David Graham, (and later the professional at Kingston Heath) remembers picking up David and another trainee in his car for a couple of rounds one Monday at Woodlands Golf Club. The idea was to play 18 holes in the morning, have a sandwich for lunch, and play another 18 holes in the afternoon. On the first hole in the morning David had a double bogey 6 and promptly retired to the practice fairway. The other two completed their 18 holes, had some lunch, and were joined at the last minute by David to play a second 18 holes. "Again David had a six on the first hole and again he stomped off to the practice fairway. After finishing our second 18 we signalled to David that we were leaving to drive home." David was still on the practice range. To their surprise he yelled back for them to go without him as he "needed to continue with his practice." Lindsay found out later that David had stayed on the practice fairway until darkness set in. Then, and only then, he lugged his golf bag over his shoulder and hitchhiked home all the way to Glen Waverley.

Ranald Macdonald, the great-grandson of the legendary Australian newspaperman, David Syme, and himself the Managing Director of *The Age* at only 26 years of age, played regularly at Riversdale in the early 1960s with David Graham.

In an interview for *Golf Victoria* magazine (April 2010), Macdonald acknowledged that back then he didn't detect in Graham the player who would become a two time major champion. "Rather immodestly", he remembered, "I felt I was a better chipper and putter than he was. We'd play for a few dollars. He was a young man of few words but always a delight to play with." Indeed Macdonald shared "a common ground" with Graham, having also switched from playing golf left-handed to right-handed as a youngster.

The author's first encounter with David Graham was a few months after David had started his apprenticeship with George Naismith. It was at the Victorian Boys Championship, played that year at Riversdale. In the locker room of the Riversdale club house there was a full size billiard table which proved to be very popular with some of the boys on completion of their rounds. On the first day of competition I watched as a young David Graham 'took on' a couple of the amateurs in a game of snooker. His challenge to them lasted only three or four minutes. The stern voice of George Naismith rang out from the doorway leaving no doubt that David's game was over. "Put the cue back in the rack laddie," instructed George, "you still have work to do in the pro shop." Without a word Graham beat a hasty retreat to the workbench.

George Naismith certainly worked the boy non-stop during the early years of his apprenticeship, giving him every job he could. Sometimes David would return home so tired he couldn't eat his dinner. He would fall on his bed and go to sleep fully clothed. He had one day off a week and on that day he would still get up at 6am and play golf all day. With long hours day after day and no weekends off, it seemed such a hard life for someone so young. His mother noted that "The more tired he was, the more determined to stick it out he became. Over time I began to see the wisdom behind this training", she said. "If his determination and ambition was to be broken it was better to do it then and let him pursue some other occupation before it was too late."

In the latter years of his apprenticeship, and early on as an assistant professional, he suffered for his outspoken ambition. He would tell everyone what he was going to do, only to be answered with laughter or ridicule. He withdrew more and more into a world of his own. He was labelled 'a loner'. He would see other assistants have late nights, skip practice, have a few drinks, but that path was not for him. He became even more determined. Frequently he would say to his mother "I'll show all of them one day, just wait and see."

When David went off to play in the assistants' competitions, usually on a Monday, with "a clean shirt and a bag almost as big as himself," Patricia Graham would send him out the front door with a "good luck Joe." According to her, it was something that stuck throughout the years. "Much later in America, his little son Andrew would say the same thing on the first morning of a tournament."

Following David Graham's first win playing as a right-hander, there was a period of renewed confidence in his golf game. Several more Monday competition wins came his way, and with it, his first mention in a newspaper article. His mother remembered the morning well.

"A few months later he was interviewed by Judy Joy Davies from 'The Sun' newspaper. When it arrived in the paper box the next morning I grabbed it out of the box and sat on the bed just staring at it. The heading said it all, 'Young Man With Drive'. To me one sentence in the back page article stood out. 'George Naismith is predicting that within a few years the youngster will be Victoria's top professional and George should know.'"

* * *

In 1962 David turned 16 years of age. It was a significant milestone for him in more ways than one. He was at that stage, the youngest ever in Victoria to be admitted to the PGA as a full professional. To celebrate this achievement the boss shouted him a trip to play in the Australian Open Championship in Adelaide, South Australia. He was looking forward to his first aeroplane flight, but after much discussion agreed to his mother's pleas to go by train. At the same time David made her realise that "plane trips, and plenty of them, were in the future" and there would be "no time to mess about," as he put it.

The plan was for Patricia not to go to Spencer Street Railway Station to see him depart. But, as it was his first trip away, at "the last minute I decided to go to the station and see David off. When I reached the platform the train was about to leave. I managed to find David in his compartment just as the train started to slowly move off. It was then that the 'Mum' in me really took over. I yelled out 'did you pack some spare underpants?' to his great embarrassment."

Soon after David won the 1977 Australian Open at the Australian Golf Club in Sydney, a young member from Riversdale telephoned Patricia to say how pleased he was with David's win because he remembered when David had played in that 1962 Open. He told her he was on the practice fairway at Riversdale when David came back from his first Open experience. Evidently he was dragging his overnight bag and golf bag up the long driveway from the front entrance to the clubhouse and pro-shop looking quite disconsolate. Patricia found out later that when he got to the pro-shop he said to George Naismith "Sorry Boss, I didn't do too well for you, but I promise I'll win it for you one day." Fifteen years later he kept his promise.

3.

"YOU'RE DIGGING A HOLE FOR YOURSELF HERE, COME WITH ME TO SYDNEY."

1988 was a year of reflection for David Graham. For one thing he thought how much easier his career in golf would have been had he known how to achieve mental toughness at a younger age. Recent successes tended to erase much of "the pain, frustration, discouragement and torment" of his early years but the reality was that most of them were "pure hell." He felt that this was due only in part to the mechanical deficiencies of his early golf swing but that a great deal of it could be traced back to "an extremely poor mental attitude" and his inability to control his emotions on the golf course.

"Many of my mental problems in golf," he noted, "can be traced to struggles in my personal life. Most of them, however, can be attributed to my not knowing how to approach the game with the right frame of mind. Like many amateurs, I knew my attitude was bad but didn't know how to go about improving it. I had a fierce temper and very little patience. I lacked composure. I was a painfully slow player, so much so that other professionals dreaded being paired with me. I was a brooder and a loner and kept to myself as much as possible. I was perpetually angry with myself and others for reasons that now seem ridiculous. In sum, I was deeply insecure and scared to death of showing emotion to anyone. This did not bode well for my game."

At the beginning of his career there was an incident that revealed how David Graham was seen by many of his fellow competitors. He had received a new golf bag from one of the equipment companies with his initials embossed on the side of the bag. Soon after he started using this bag he discovered that one, or more, of these competitors, had used a black marker pen to neatly print the letter O between the D and the G.

For much of his early years David Graham waged a battle, not just with other golfers, spectators and officials, but with himself. Yet his anger, frustration and sheer desperation served to make him incredibly determined. In his book, 'Mental Toughness Training for Golf', he wrote. "I practised harder than anyone, studied the game diligently, and was utterly single-minded in my purpose to become a good player. After about 10 years this approach began to pay off. But what a price I paid! Had I known all I know now about managing myself as well as my golf game, I'm convinced I would have tasted success much earlier, at a much lower price. Significantly, it was my win in the 1981 US Open Championship at Merion Golf Club that signalled the end of my long and torturous battle within myself."

Even earlier, a major turning point in David's life was the resignation, in 1963, of George Naismith from Riversdale Golf Club. It was a sudden departure by Naismith after more than thirty years at the club. Fiercely loyal to his family and close friends it is believed that some derogatory remarks made to George by a committeeman about his (Naismith's) de facto wife sparked a heated exchange between the two and Naismith's subsequent resignation. This left David with "nowhere to go." Realising this, George arranged for David, at the tender age of just 17, to take the professional job at Seabrook Golf Club, a nine-hole course in Tasmania.

In David's words, "It didn't take long for me to go stone broke there. I knew nothing about retailing and ordered too much equipment. I was persuaded to purchase a car that I couldn't afford. I sank about AU$6,000 into debt and became utterly depressed. I thought the world was against me."

"I still have a very big chip on my shoulder, I guess you might call it, after my days of being in Tasmania. My apprenticeship days working for George Naismith at Riversdale were some of my happier memories but my couple of years at Seabrook were absolutely miserable. I felt I was a young guy trying to get ahead and here I was on a little nine-hole course and all of these so-called wealthy people were playing golf there. Had it not been for two men, NSW professional Eric Cremin, and Precision Golf Forgings (PGF) Chairman, Claire Higson, God only knows where I would have been financially in Tasmania."

* * *

Chapter 3

Eric Cremin went to Tasmania as a representative of the major Australian golf club manufacturer, PGF, and also to play a series of exhibition matches. When he went to Seabrook, David had to play an 18-hole match with him. David admitted to being as "nervous as a kitten in a doghouse" as they teed off. He played well despite his nerves and after the game Cremin took him aside. "Son, you're a pretty good player," he said. "You've got to get out of this place. You're digging a hole for yourself here that you might never get out of. It's a waste of time. Come with me to Sydney and I'll get you a job with our golf company."

David knew he was right. "I sold the equipment in the shop, packed my bags and headed to Sydney. I met with Tom McKay, a Sydney businessman and now a close friend, and he guaranteed that he would pay off my Tasmanian debts while I, in turn, would pay him back out of my pay cheques. I paid it all back, but it took me a couple of years at least. For 18 months after arriving in Sydney I never went out. I lived on fish and chips and baked beans."

His work at PGF consisted mainly of doing errands, but he also learned how to balance and swing-weight clubs and custom-fit them for people. These skills were to be much appreciated in later years by three major winners, Jack Nicklaus, Gary Player and Ian Baker-Finch.

As for playing, his tournaments were limited to Monday pro-ams. Eventually he graduated to what became known as 'The Troppo Tour' or more formally The Queensland Tour. But, according to Graham, that's where "my life hit rock bottom."

Many years later it was still painful for David to look back on those days. "I was still in debt from my Tasmanian job, my game was awful and emotionally I was a miserable wreck. I had less natural ability than anyone on the circuit and was reminded of this often by players and outsiders. My self-esteem was very low. While other players received such perks as lessons, free clubs, and balls, I couldn't even find a place to practise. I wound up spending 90 percent of my time practising on a shabby football field, where I was kicked off regularly for hitting the balls too far over the field onto a road."

David did manage "a few nice finishes" on the Queensland circuit but realistically knew that if nothing changed he had little chance of succeeding in the ranks of professional tournament golf. It seemed to him that nobody was willing to help him but he didn't know how to help himself either.

He described himself in this way. "The depth of my despair is difficult for most people to comprehend, especially people who have never been in my situation. I came close to quitting a hundred times. I was forever being told things like, 'You're too small.' 'You're not strong enough.' 'You have no talent.' 'Your swing is no good.' 'Find something else to do.' It was one thing not to have any encouragement but quite another to have to endure constant criticism from people who wouldn't think of offering any help."

All of the put-downs and negative comments made him respond with more physical effort. "Somehow I sensed that if I worked harder than anyone else I would, eventually, be rewarded for it. I became an utter workaholic at golf. I worked on my game every day, all day long. Nobody can stand on a practice range from sunup to sundown, of course, but a typical day would start with me chipping and putting when the sun came up, followed by eighteen holes. I'd eat some fish and chips for lunch, play eighteen more holes, then hit balls until I was exhausted. Then I would go chip and putt some more. I'd drag myself home, fall into bed, get up the next day, and do it all over again."

That insatiable appetite for practice never stopped. More than once he would hit balls until blisters developed on his hands. After they'd burst he would practise some more, even beyond the point when they would start bleeding. The result was the development of a swing that was somewhat unnatural looking but rigidly effective.

* * *

Colin de Groot, the much respected teaching professional at Pymble Golf Club in Sydney, remembers "Once when he came to see me for tuition I asked him what he wanted out of golf. 'To become a world champion', he said. The look in his eyes told me he meant exactly what he said." De Groot went on to give what remains as one of the best descriptions of the David Graham golf swing, "it is very mechanical but as methodical as a metronome, never missing a beat."

David Graham's work ethic is evident in this story concerning the Junior Interstate Teams Competition held every year over the Easter holiday period. In 1966 the series was held at Forbes in New South Wales. David accompanied a fellow PGF employee on the trip to Forbes. He watched little of the golf over the four days, preferring instead to spend most of each day on the practice fairway. Significantly, he took only one club along with his bag of well-worn practice balls, his wedge. Even at that early age he recognised the importance of wedge play if he was to succeed as a professional golfer.

David Graham was acutely aware that due to his lack of a formal education if he failed at golf he would, as he put it, "be in serious trouble." Total prize money for pro-ams was not usually any more than AU$500. First prize was a cheque for about AU$100 and David "needed that money in the worst possible way." Talking about this pressure years later, he admitted that he began to regard every shot as a life or death proposition, which in a way, it was.

"I was chronically slow. I would mark six-inch putts and would hold up the whole field because the thought of blowing a putt and losing a few dollars was too dire to consider. I had a violent temper, throwing clubs all the time and arguing with every person in sight. Socially I came off as cocky and arrogant. I needed help with my game, with my finances, with my mental attitude. But at this point, nobody wanted to listen."

Mechanically he felt his game was inadequate. His swing had been largely self-taught. It was flat, wristy, and produced anything from a draw to a low hook. Not surprisingly it didn't hold up very well under pressure. "I got the ball into the hole by sheer force of will. Physically, I was terribly intimidated by other players. I weighed 132 pounds (60kg) and had a twenty-eight inch (71cm) waist. I gradually built myself up by exercising religiously. One time I damn near killed myself when I accidentally dropped a set of barbells on my head."

Still haunted by debts incurred during his time at Seabrook, the mental side of his game continued to suffer. As well, his slow play, poor on-course manners, and a tendency to complain to everyone about everything, made him very unpopular with other players. In his 1988 book he wrote of those dark times in a frank and refreshingly open way.

"I had more feelings of failure than I can express. For years these feelings manifested in strange ways. When I later played the Asian Tour, for instance, I used to fake being sick if I had a bad round. I was always making excuses. This is hard for me to admit now. If I made a friend, I'd lose him right away by starting some silly argument. I refused to socialise with people. Instead of going to the beach or to parties, I virtually lived at the golf course and in my hotel. I had no sense of caring for others, no sense of humor, no zest for living."

David's first year on the Queensland Tour was highly significant in his battle with these inner demons. At the Cairns Open he met Maureen Burdett. During that week they went out a few times but he didn't see her again until the tour returned to Cairns the following year. David knew very early on that Maureen was someone very special. He proposed, she accepted and they married soon after. "At last", he said, "I had found someone I could trust and someone I felt cared for me. Her presence seemed to remove some of the immense pressure I placed on myself."

Back in Melbourne, David's mother was, over the ensuing years, to recognise the vital role played by Maureen in David's personal, let alone professional, development. She wrote in 1979, "Just when a lot was stacked against David, into his life came the one person so essential. When all the chips were down, that person simply had faith in him and gave him the reason to tackle everything before him. Her belief in him was the one thing he really needed at that stage. That person was his wife Maureen. Right from the outset, Maureen was prepared to travel and live out of a suitcase. Always staying quietly in the background, never seeking publicity, she was a very special person."

Soon after returning to Sydney from Queensland, David developed a close working relationship with two of the finest golfers and teachers Australia has produced, Norman Von Nida and Alex Mercer. Aware of David Graham's obsession with practice, and then more practice, Mercer gave him this piece of timely advice on one of the occasional fishing trips they took. "David, you've got to get away like this more often. You can't eat, sleep, and drink golf. You've got to take a break." David's reply says much about his mindset at that and many other times. He didn't really understand what Mercer was saying. "Why?", he asked Mercer. In fact he refused to go fishing with him again unless it was after 8.00pm, "when it was too dark to practise golf."

4.

"THE OFFICIALS WANTED ME TO GIVE THE TROPHY BACK"

David Graham's first tournament win over seventy-two holes was in the 1967 Queensland PGA Championship shortly after his twenty-first birthday. He won with a 10 under par total of 282. Although important, it was the Australian PGA Championship of 1968 that really marked his entry into the upper levels of tournament golf.

Graham shot a six under par 68 on the second day to move into contention. The quality of the field at the Metropolitan Golf Club that year far exceeded that of the Queensland PGA a year earlier. In addition to top Australian players, Thomson, Nagle, Devlin, Dunk among others, a trio of famous overseas golfers, namely Jack Nicklaus, Gary Player and Arnold Palmer teed up.

Early in the third round on Saturday, Graham got a birdie and at the very next hole, sank a long putt for what he, and the exuberant gallery, thought was another birdie. The problem was that the caddie

On the way to winning the 1967 Queensland PGA Championship by 5 shots.

didn't pull out the flagstick in time and Graham's ball grazed the pin before disappearing into the cup. In golf that is an automatic two-stroke penalty. David sank to his knees and dropped his putter so he could bury his head in his hands. There his two hands stayed for quite a few seconds. They were hiding the tears running down his cheeks. He didn't get over the setback and quickly slid to a 77. During the final round, in the company of Arnold Palmer, he displayed the fighting spirit that was to become one of his trademarks to fire a three under par 71. It was enough to secure a share of sixth place. The following week he was most definitely a winner. He flew to Cairns to marry Maureen Burdett who he had met while playing the tropical tour in Queensland a year earlier and with whom he had kept in touch ever since.

1969 proved to be another significant year both on and off the golf course. It was the year that his employer (PGF) selected him to represent them on the Asian Golf Tour. PGF had an incentive program for young in-house staff members. As a reward for winning some of the regular Monday pro-ams, the company would provide an airline ticket to play on the Asian Tour. After several Monday wins early in 1969, Graham was the recipient of one of those airline tickets.

PGF's sponsorship was limited to paying David's airfares but, with the company's assistance, he kept his living costs down by finding accommodation in a string of local family homes all over the circuit.

After a promising start in the Philippines he 'struck pay-dirt' in Singapore. Playing in the Singapore Open he tied for first place, storming home with a 63 in the final round. In the sudden death play off he lost on the third extra hole but the runner-up cheque of US$2,000 seemed, to the young professional, "like an absolute fortune." He had another second placing in Malaysia and followed that with a fifth place at the Hong Kong Open.

Returning to Australia, David Graham teed up in the 1969 Dunlop International at the Yarra Yarra Golf Club in Melbourne's famous 'sand-belt'. The tournament boasted, as its two main drawcards, the American golfers, Lee Trevino and Orville Moody. Trevino, who, for some reason, used the small British ball on the par three and par five holes but the larger American ball on all of the par four holes, joked his way around all four days to finish in a tie with Bruce Devlin. Devlin promptly won the tournament with a birdie on the first play-off hole.

Chapter 4

David Graham finished well back, yet of significance that week was his meeting with Bucky Woy, the flamboyant, fast talking manager of Trevino and Moody who he had accompanied on this trip of Australia. Graham succumbed to the persuasive entreaties of Woy and signed up for the American to manage his off-course affairs for the next five years. Graham was convinced that this move would go a long way to relieving him of the organisational and financial pressures that afflict most young players, especially those with overseas golfing ambitions.

In a letter to George Naismith, 16 December 1969 (Appendix I), Graham indicated his relief at signing the contract with Woy for the American circuit. "He also will be sponsoring me to the Far East, England, and the Continent and to make the arrangement even better he has guaranteed the expenses for my wife also. The New Zealand circuit is going smoothly although I am not winning a great deal of money this is probably owing to the fact that I have been worrying about confirmation of my new contract, now that it has been confirmed, I hope that I can now settle down again and play some good golf."

With the relative stability of this management contract, and practising harder than ever before, he went on a scoring spree in 1970 that netted him two, and almost three, state open championships in just under a month.

* * *

The state opens were much bigger events in the seventies than they are now with high quality fields and considerable media attention. The first victory was in the Tasmanian Open. Coincidentally his wining total was exactly the same as his first tournament win back in 1964, a 10 under par 282. Graham won AU$1,000 and, at the presentation, thought it was time for him to reveal a sense of humour.

He explains it this way. "Billy Dunk, a prolific winner of many pro-ams, had a famous line which he would often bring out in his acceptance speech. 'Ladies and gentlemen, small cheque, small speech, thank you.' Billy was very well liked by players and fans, and this line always got a big laugh. Billy wasn't in that field in Tasmania so I borrowed his speech word for word, all nine of them, and then promptly sat back down again. Well, you could have heard a pin drop and the next morning the officials summoned me for a dressing down. They even wanted me to give the trophy back. I wrote a letter of apology to the Tasmanian Golf Association and Peter Thomson convinced them not to take any action. I kept the trophy and 40 years on I still have it, my first open championship trophy, at home with me in America."

The following week the tour crossed Bass Strait for the Victorian Open. Significantly it was played at Riversdale Golf Club. Mike Clayton, well known golf professional and course architect, was in the gallery at Riversdale and has since written about the final round.

"One of the first tournaments I watched was the 1970 Victorian Open at Riversdale. Riversdale was a good course then, although it played as a very vulnerable par 73. Graham shot something like twenty under for the four rounds.

In the final round, at the long par five fifteenth, Graham was a shot ahead of the best amateur in the country, Kevin Hartley, but Hartley had pitched to only four feet and David had a twenty-footer for his birdie. Graham made the putt, Hartley missed, and the tournament was as good as over."

It was Graham's first return to Riversdale since the acrimonious departure of his 'Boss' and his own sudden 'transfer' to Tasmania seven years earlier. The win, in front of the many members who had supported and encouraged him through his teenage years, must have given him great satisfaction. No doubt his mentor George Naismith would have loved to be there when he sank the final putt right in front of the old pro-shop in which they shared so many memories. However relations between Naismith and some of the club officials were still strained and he stayed at home.

Writing to Naismith in April 1970 (Appendix I), soon after his Victorian Open triumph, Graham said. "I saw and met many of the members who were there back in the good old days. It was quite funny to me because at first they didn't really care whether they spoke to me or not but on Sunday night, I found that I had more friends than I knew what to do with. I guess I'm tarred with the same brush as you. I am referring to the fact that my memory is not that short."

A fortnight after the Victorian Open, in the New South Wales Open, David Graham tied with Frank Phillips after 72 holes by birdying 5 of the last 6 holes of the last round. In the 18 hole play-off the next day Phillips won by 3 shots.

Spurred on by these performances, David Graham again tackled the Asian Tour where more success followed. He won the Thailand Open and then, in late April, the Yomiuri International in Japan. There he banked a cheque for US$7,500 and also won a car. To cap it all off, he collected a US$10,000 bonus for being the leading money winner in Asia for 1970.

In June of 1970 David Graham was a house guest of Bucky Woy whose Consulting Services Inc. was sponsoring him on tour. Interviewed by the local newspaper, *The Akron Beacon Journal*, the young 24-year old Australian outlined his aim "to play here in America. If I want to be

Purposefully striding across the second green after holing a long putt during the 4th round of the 1970 Victorian Open at Riversdale GC. Photo courtesy Golf in Victoria.

a great golfer then I must play the Palmer's and the Nicklaus's but more than that, I want to prove I can be consistently good all over the world."

But all was not well. Nearly two decades later Graham was able to candidly reflect on those Asian Tour experiences. In his book "Mental Toughness Training for Golf" he wrote. "Despite the slight improvement in my self-perception and outlook on life, my behaviour on the Asian Tour was in many ways abominable and reflected my inner torment. I was still my own worst enemy, on and off the golf course. I used to scream at the bus driver for wanting to shuttle the players back to the hotel at 4pm when, as I saw it, there was plenty of daylight left to practise. I continued to work like the devil. I was always the last one to leave the practice range, and to my way of thinking, there wasn't enough time in the day for me to get the practice I needed."

"I felt that the only way to earn respect and attention was to play and practise harder. At this point I could afford, as a result of my winnings, to have Maureen join me in Asia. One day she asked me, 'David, why do you act so badly on the golf course when you're a totally different person off it? Why do people dislike you when I think you're a very nice person?' My feeble answer was, It helps me play better. But I knew it wasn't true."

David Graham's hunger for practice was matched by his appetite for competition. In this respect, these words of Sam Snead at the 1972 US Masters hold true for a young 24 year old David Graham in 1970. Snead, then aged 80, said "No, I can't say it was fun (shooting a round of 69). There was blood on every shot. But I do like the competition, mixing it up with them." A few months after his lucrative sojourn through Asia, David travelled to Europe for the first time. There he captured the prestigious French Open Championship closing with another blistering final round, this time a 64. These sub-par final rounds were to become something of a Graham specialty whenever he was in contention to win. This was especially evident in 1979 at Oakland Hills and, two years later, at Merion Golf Club.

Brimming with what he later labelled "a bad case of over-confidence" he travelled to the USA towards the end of 1970 to try and qualify for the 1971 PGA Tour. He didn't play well in the qualifying rounds and missed out. It was a major setback to his ambitions but whilst still regretting his poor form, a very positive thing happened a couple of days later.

* * *

In 1970 the International Golf Association wanted Bruce Crampton to be Bruce Devlin's playing partner in the World Cup at the Jockey Club in Buenos Aires, Argentina. The Australian PGA dug its heels in and threatened not to send a team if David Graham, the best locally based player, wasn't included. The IGA relented and Graham was on his way to Argentina.

As it turned out, fate had dealt him a trump card. The combination of Devlin and Graham streeted the high class field of international golfers, winning by ten strokes, and setting a (then) tournament record low score of 544. So well did David Graham play that he finished runner up to local hero Roberto de Vicenzo in the concurrent individual competition. He probably should have won because after three brilliant rounds of 65, 67 and 65 he had an uncharacteristic fade out on the fourth day to record a one over par 73. Cheered on by a fanatically enthusiastic home crowd, de Vicenzo stormed home to pip Graham by just one stroke. Nevertheless it was a wonderful four days. "I flew down to Argentina in coach (second) class but flew back in first class," he said later.

The World Cup win was greeted with much enthusiasm in Australia. David's mother "drove all over Melbourne" the night after their victory in the Cup just to see his (and Devlin's) name on the headline sheets that stood outside the newsagents and milk bars.

The World Cup in Argentina was important for David Graham in one other way. During their time together in Buenos Aires, Graham and Devlin struck up a close and enduring friendship. According to Graham "it was my first close exposure to a world class golfer. Bruce Devlin was everything I was not. A tremendous player, a well-liked person and someone who handled everything with incredible grace and composure. I admired him immensely and wanted to be more like him."

Soon after winning the World Cup, Devlin told Graham that he "would be mad" if he didn't try to qualify for the US Tour again. Graham had played the Asian Tour for the past two years but did not enjoy it despite his successes. "It was not an organised tour like today," he recalled several years ago. "My wife and I had no children then, so we packed up and went to the States and settled in Florida."

David Graham and Bruce Devlin were again selected to represent Australia and defend their title in the 1971 World Cup. This time they finished several places behind the winning USA team, whose members were the formidable Jack Nicklaus and Lee Trevino.

When Bruce Devlin was left out of the 1972 World Cup pairing, David Graham, who had been selected, refused to play. He felt Devlin had done an outstanding job in the previous two World Cups and wanted no part of a team that excluded him. True to his word, David Graham never represented Australia in any subsequent World Cups.

David Graham did represent Australia on two other occasions, namely the 1985 and 1986 Dunhill Cups. In the inaugural 1985 Dunhill Cup he teamed with Greg Norman and Graham Marsh. The trio proved to be well-chosen as they won the Cup, played at St Andrews, by demolishing the USA team 3 matches to nil in the final.

Reaching the final was more of a cut-throat affair however and only a piece of David Graham brilliance got them there. In the semi-final against Wales, with the contest standing at one individual match each, Graham and his Welsh opponent, Ian Woosnam, stood all square on the seventeenth tee in the deciding match. After a good drive over the corner of this famous 'road-hole' Graham was left with a mid-iron second shot to the narrow green. David's perfectly struck five-iron drew slightly to land a fraction short of the green, but on the right line. From there it bounced on to the front of the green and ran up to within a few inches of the hole. An elated Greg Norman emerged from the gallery to congratulate Graham, knowing full well the significance of the shot in the overall context of the semi-final. Conspicuous by his absence at this point was the third Australian team member, Graham Marsh, for reasons that will be revealed later.

David Graham's 'kick-in' birdie won the hole and, when both players halved the eighteenth hole, Australia was through to the final by the barest of margins. Many of those who witnessed that five iron shot either on the course or via television reckon it to be amongst the very best ever played on St Andrews seventeenth during the crucial stages of a major tournament.

5.

"I THOUGHT I WAS A BIGSHOT. REALLY, I DIDN'T KNOW THE FIRST THING ABOUT THE GAME."

David Graham and Graham Marsh were at loggerheads during the 1985 Dunhill Cup Tournament over the issue of appearance money paid to overseas based Australian players invited to Australian tournaments. This issue had long been a thorn in David Graham's side. In fact he refused to play in the 1982 Australian Open in protest at the PGA's policy of not paying 'big name' Australian players to compete in Australia. This antagonism between Graham and Marsh did not go unnoticed. One British newspaper carried an article headed 'Aussies at War'. By the same token the article recognised that "in the euphoria of one of the all-time great Australian team victories, pride in personal achievement and pride for their country had carried the day." It had been impossible to keep the row between Graham and Marsh under wraps. Prior to the 1985 Dunhill Cup, Marsh had publicly condemned David Graham for accepting what he considered to be excessive appearance money for the Queensland Open. Marsh, a senior member of the Australian PGA, was fully supportive of the PGA's policy that Australian players should not receive appearance money.

According to Jack Newton, Graham "was getting at least AU$10,000 every time he stepped foot in the country." These payments, which started in the late seventies and continued well into the eighties, were 'justified' on the basis that Graham was domiciled in the USA and therefore eligible for the appearance money. Players like Newton and Bob Shearer who spent up to ten months a year overseas, yet didn't 'qualify' for appearance fees, were decidedly disadvantaged by this arrangement.

The issue came to a head in 1980 when several Australian players threatened to boycott that year's Australian Open. One of them was

Melbourne's favourite golfing son, Bob Shearer, who had also threatened to stay away from the previous year's Australian PGA

David Graham did receive some support from an unlikely source, Greg Norman. Norman claimed that "players can't bitch about what the sponsor wants to do with his money." Norman believed that "Australian players should get appearance money if they have proven themselves. Bob's won nothing really big yet but David Graham has won an Australian Open, proved himself in America and has also won the World Match Play Championship." Suffice to say the whole appearance fee debate was still unresolved five years later at the inaugural Dunhill Cup.

Comments made by the three Australian team members on the eve of their first match in the Cup, helped clarify their respective feelings.

David Graham, still irate at Marsh's public denigration of him, told *The Edinburgh Evening News*, "Graham Marsh may well be hearing from my lawyer."

Graham Marsh, for his part, noted that "It's a good job we're playing as individuals this week, not as partners."

Greg Norman, caught in the middle of this dispute and, probably, seeing both sides of the argument, was also thankful that "we are playing each of the matches separately, not strictly as a team, otherwise I don't know what would have happened."

Reflecting on those years of protest about appearance money, David Graham feels that there was a lot more jealousy within the ranks of Australian players back then. "If someone like myself came back and got two free tickets with Qantas, a hotel room and, maybe, a AU$15,000 appearance fee, there was high resentment. Even when Palmer, Nicklaus and Player used to come for the Australian Open and they got, say, a AU$20,000 fee, everyone was screaming bloody blue murder. They said that the money should have been in the prize money and that we didn't need Nicklaus, Palmer and Player." Graham has always considered such a viewpoint as unrealistic. "Those three made the Australian Open, they made any tournament that they played in. In truth golf should be indebted to them for going all over the world playing golf."

In the modern era it is Tiger Woods and Phil Mickelson and the emerging Northern Irishman, Rory McIlroy, who are the major drawcards, but the scenario is the same. "Without them you don't have a really big tournament," Graham said recently. "It's been the same old argument for fifty years and I don't think it will ever go away."

* * *

The following year, Graham and Norman again represented Australia although this time the third team member was Rodger Davis. Australia won the Dunhill Cup with David Graham winning three out of his four matches.

Returning to 1971, David Graham added two more victories to his ever-expanding resume, the Caracas Open and the Japan Airlines Open. At the age of twenty-five he had already won tournaments, quite literally all over the world, from Japan in the north to Australia in the south and from France in Europe to Venezuela and Argentina on the other side of the globe. What was missing from this list was a win on American soil.

Earlier in that year he had taken the most important step towards correcting this omission. He had returned to the US PGA qualifying school but, unlike his first attempt, twelve months previously, he played consistently and well. He secured his PGA tour card by a comfortable margin.

David Graham had only moderate success in his first full year on the PGA Tour. He finished well down on the money list, in 135th place. That rather disappointing result brought back the self-doubt that, irrespective of his wins outside America, was still never far from the surface. He felt that "after eight years as a professional, working on my game virtually full time, neither my golf swing nor my mental attitude were good enough for me to compete against the very best players in the world." This feeling of inadequacy was reinforced on his first trip to the US Masters in April 1971.

At Augusta he played horribly. "I thought I was a big shot, but after I played one round in the Masters I found I really didn't know the first thing about the game. I couldn't spin the ball… I didn't know how to hit it high… and if you can't do that in the States you're dead." The game of golf, according to David Feherty, now a golf commentator on American television, "is just a mirror, that's all it is." As David Graham was now finding out "your weaknesses glare at you in the face." Graham knew that his stock shot, "a low, running, looping hook", was only good on "a links-style course in forty miles (64km) an hour winds."

In despair Graham asked Bruce Devlin to come down to Colonial Country Club, in Texas, and watch him hit some balls. Graham has never forgotten it. After about 20 balls Devlin said to him, "Do you want the good news, the bad news or do you want it all at once?" David Graham replied, "Give it all to me." "Then he started," said Graham. "He said, 'You stand too far away from the ball. Your clubs are too flat. Your left hand is too strong. Your right hand is too far under the club, and that's the reason you hit these sling-hooks all the time.' So I set about changing the entire way I played golf." The way he eventually learned to do it was to take a bucket of balls and a 5-iron and stand behind a tree he knew he couldn't clear with his old swing. "I would stand there and make all of these changes with my grip and try to get the clubface square and the shaft more on the line, until eventually I could hit up over that tree. I rebuilt my entire game. It took me about two years to get it all right."

During that two-year building phase David Graham actually broke through for his first victory on the US PGA Tour. His win in the Cleveland Open of 1972 had an ironic twist to it. With a higher ball trajectory, that is so essential in the target golf of the PGA Tour, he played well enough to tie for first on 278 at the end of 72 holes. The player he then beat on the 2nd play-off hole was none other than the man who had put him on to the path of a higher ball flight, Bruce Devlin.

The rumour still circulates in the golfing world that Bruce Devlin let David Graham beat him in the play-off for that event to restore Graham's confidence. Going through a difficult period in America, David Graham was on the point of returning to Australia when he won in Cleveland. It is highly unlikely that there is any truth to this rumour, but it is certain that the victory in Ohio set Graham on a path that was to take him to the very top of his profession.

What is also true is that his friendship with Devlin, who Graham often described as being "like an older brother", helped transform David from the bad-tempered anxious young man he had been for so long. Terry Smith, writing in the *Sydney Morning Herald* in 1979, saw David Graham's life as one that was very confused. "His thirty-three years have been split between careers as a golf club designer and as a player, between the heights of tournament success and the depths of financial misery and between an embittered adolescence and a generous open maturity."

Gaining confidence all the time in his rebuilt swing, Graham had a number of other good results and, by season's end, had climbed to thirty-fifth in the money list. This was exactly one hundred places further up from where he had finished the previous year, his first on the Tour.

* * *

David Graham won more than $US150,000 worldwide in the 1972 calendar year. His improved finances enabled him to buy his way out of the five-year management contract (signed in 1969) with Bucky Woy. Graham was unhappy with the American's management style and was anxious to sever his connection with him. The termination with Woy, mid-contract, proved to be very costly (in excess of US$200,000) and was a salutory lesson for the young Australian regarding all future business arrangements.

Jack Newton, colourful as ever, summed it up this way. "Bucky Woy was a Yank who gave David an American Express card, but when David started winning, the 60-40 split, or whatever it was, became a very expensive proposition."

By this time David Graham was forging a reputation as a steely competitor, especially 'down the stretch' in the final round of a tournament and in the pressure packed atmosphere of a play-off. Yet 1972 was notable for two play-off losses, one in Japan and the other in Australia.

Playing in Tokyo at the Taiheyo Masters he bogied the first extra hole of the sudden-death play-off to lose to the American golfer, Gay Brewer. He missed out on the $US65,000 first prize, settling instead for an acceptable second place cheque of $US32,500. These substantial amounts demonstrated the significant difference between tournament prize money overseas and that paid out in Australia. At the Taiheyo Masters the total prize money was $US300,000. By contrast the Chrysler Classic, played the following year at the Lakes Course in Sydney, was billed at that time as Australia's richest ever golf tournament. The total prize pool was $AU50,000.

* * *

The 1972 Australian Open was played at Adelaide's Kooyonga Golf Club and Sydney based golf writer, Terry Smith, summarised the first four rounds in these words. "Graham, consumed with ambition for greatness, took over at the halfway mark with a 69 and was so confident of winning his first Open that he rang his wife Maureen, who was visiting her mother in Cairns, and told her to catch the first plane to Adelaide. Graham was still in front after Saturday's third-round 70. Entering the final day he was one ahead of Thomson, who had shot a third-round 68."

Amid great excitement in the final round, Thomson played a three-quarter strength seven iron to only 10 inches (25cm) from the cup on the 72nd hole. His tap-in birdie gave him a total of 281. Graham needed to finish birdie then par to win, but it was beyond him. He finished par, par, holing a three-footer (1metre) putt at the last to force the play-off.

Asked who would win, third place getter, British player Maurice Bembridge, predicted: 'If Graham plays his best golf, he'll win but if it develops into a waiting game, there can only be one winner – Peter Thomson.'

Nine years earlier, when Peter Thomson had four British Opens to his credit, a nervous young sixteen-year old named David Graham went to Victoria Golf Club in Melbourne to play with him. George Naismith arranged the game. "I guess serving my time with the same professional as Peter Thomson did, had a big effect on me then" Graham said prior to the 1972 Open play-off. "That game with Peter was a big stepping stone in my life. I remember thinking this is a big deal."

Certainly the Monday play-off was a big deal for George Naismith. Speaking on radio he said, "It's a big day for me. It's not often that two of your boys fight out for the big one." George planned to listen to the progress scores of the play-off as they came through. "I intended to send a telegram this morning, but then I thought I should send two, so finally I decided I wouldn't send any."

On the morning of the play-off, the preparations for the 'fifth round' by the two protagonists could not have been more different. David Graham arrived early to pound ball after ball down the practice fairway as was his custom. Peter Thomson on the other hand hit no more than a dozen or so practice balls just to be sure he was "finding the middle of the bat." The concluding part of Thomson's pre-match routine was to have a cup of tea whilst relaxing on the clubhouse verandah.

Chapter 5

At the appointed starting time, and with both players now standing beside the first tee, Thomson calmly walked across to the tee markers, teed up his golf ball, and knocked it straight down the middle of the fairway. David Graham was visibly upset by this opening gambit of Thomson's. He claimed later that he was waiting for the customary toss of the coin to determine who would have the honour in such circumstances.

There is no doubt that Graham had a case but there was no recall of Thomson's ball. Clearly unsettled, David Graham proceeded to hit a big looping hook which ended up from where he had just come, the practice fairway. The problem was that in regulation play the practice fairway was out of bounds. Further gamesmanship, if we can call it that, saw Thomson hit his second shot up the fairway to about fifty yards from the green at the same time as Graham was trudging back to the tee to play what would be his third stroke. Ten minutes later Thomson holed his short birdie putt for four and when Graham could only manage a seven an immediate three-stroke advantage was opened up.

David Graham matched par for the remaining seventeen holes but it wasn't enough. Thomson, playing soundly and putting with confidence, extended his lead. The play-off ended with Peter Thomson carding a 68 to David Graham's 74.

A distinguished visitor to the Australian Open that year was Pat Ward-Thomas, the golf writer for the English newspaper, *The Guardian*. Writing in that newspaper he summed up the difference between the two golfers in this way. "There is always a sense of tension about David Graham's dark, slender figure. In his walk, manner and style, the contrast with Peter Thomson's poised, relaxed appearance was marked."

For many years David Graham and Peter Thomson enjoyed a professional relationship that, at best, could be described as a grudging acceptance of each other. To what extent the events of that 1972 October morning had on their strained relationship is difficult to gauge, but suffice to say, it remained a sore point with David Graham for many years. Yet, speaking in 2011, Graham indicated that he would like to tell Peter Thomson "what a fantastic influence he had on my life. Unfortunately, I have never said that to him in person."

Irrespective of his personal feelings towards Thomson, David Graham, in his honest and pragmatic way, answered this question, posed to him for a golf magazine article, in 1990. The question asked "Who do you think has been Australia's greatest golfer?"

"That is the easiest question in the world to answer," replied Graham, "Peter Thomson has been Australia's greatest player. You can't use money won as a yardstick because Thomson won only £500 for his first British Open win. Now (in 1990) the winner gets something like £180,000. The gauge must be majors won and Peter stands out with five of them. I would put Greg Norman number two for all that he has achieved and for what he has done for golf in this country and I think I could put myself at number three."

6.

"LEARNING TO PLAY GOLF INSTEAD OF GOLF PLAYING ME"

In the aftermath of the 1972 Australian Open play-off, David Graham was very clear on two things. The rebuilding of his swing was still a work in progress and mentally he "was the same desperate person." The intense work on the practice range continued and although the years 1973 and 1974 did not yield any significant victories, he was satisfied that the major swing change, initiated at Colonial Golf Club by Bruce Devlin, had transformed him into "a pretty fair ball striker." Improving his mental attitude, especially his perception of himself and those he came in contact with as a professional golfer, was a much longer, and more difficult, process. Two incidents from those years serve to illustrate this.

Once, on tour in South America, he engaged an entire hotel staff in a running battle over his breakfast. Starting with the kitchen hands and waitresses, who couldn't understand English anyway, the dispute continued up the chain of command to the hotel's management. The point of difference was whether Graham's eggs had been cooked for two minutes or two and a half minutes!

Living in Florida, and with a reputation as a club-maker of considerable ability and knowledge, he was asked by a neighbour for some advice on the design of MacGregor golf clubs. The neighbour was Jack Nicklaus. Jack invited David to attend a meeting of MacGregor executives. Soon after the meeting started, the president of the company made some erroneous, and rather innocuous, comments about club design. To his and everyone else's surprise, David Graham suddenly blurted out, "You have no idea what you're talking about. Why the hell did you ask me up here if you don't want my opinion."

In 1974, and almost two years since his last tournament win, David Graham "got serious" and began working on his mental attitude in earnest. "I have to learn to play golf instead of golf playing me," he said. As he remarked in 1988, "The search for more self-control was puzzling. There were no sports psychologists on the PGA Tour at that time and it was up to me to sort it out for myself."

Something David Graham did do was listen to the top players and read stories about them and, in particular, "about the techniques they used to feel comfortable and controlled on the golf course, how they were able to maintain their concentration and composure so they could play to their full potential."

Of all the top players of the seventies it was from Jack Nicklaus that Graham learnt the most. Watching Nicklaus on the range reinforced the need for him to develop and then diligently practise a pre-shot routine. Graham made sure that even during very long sessions on the practice fairway he would perform his pre-shot routine 'by the numbers'. He would count off the number of seconds he would stand over the ball, look down the target line, etc. before taking the club back. The idea was that constant repetition would make it automatic and deeply fix this element of control into his game.

David Graham also noticed that during a tournament round Jack Nicklaus appeared to be concentrating all the time, often for more than four hours at a time. By careful observation of Nicklaus and other top professionals he realised that most of them were employing passive concentration. Specifically, this means that they start to really focus their concentration to an intense level only when they reach their golf ball (or tee up) and prepare to play a shot. Graham adopted the Nicklaus method of 'total involvement in other relevant matters' in between shots. You haven't 'switched off' but instead spend the time examining the wind, the condition of the course, the way it is playing that day, how you feel physically and where you stand in the round and in the tournament as a whole.

Writing in *Golf Digest* magazine in 1991, Nicklaus spoke of this concept of 'total involvement'. "When I play golf I have to make the world revolve around me. If you want to be the best at something you have to make it revolve around what you are doing. It's that clear."

Graham even thought about copying the 'Nicklaus stare'. "I'm going to get me one of those stares like Jack", he told his wife. He really didn't need to as David Graham's game-day face had always been tight lipped with his eyes focused and unblinking.

Throughout this period Graham resolved to be more like Nicklaus in one other crucial way. Of all the Nicklaus traits, this one required the most effort. For as long as he could remember, David's bad temper had frequently brought him undone on the golf course. Jack Nicklaus on the other hand let nothing upset him or disturb his concentration during the course of a tournament round. Graham decided he would try and show little or no emotion when he got a bad break, "even if my insides felt like a kitchen blender." To say he was able to bring his temper under control would be an overstatement but his fellow professionals and even some of the caddies and spectators in the galleries did notice an improvement in his reaction to bad breaks and bad golf shots.

With Maureen in The Herald *of 30 October 1972, "Graham Lives A Dream".*

Off the course he made real progress as well. Some practice rounds in Florida were now played with friends, rather than on his own. He even began to enjoy a glass of wine now and then. Until then he had never touched alcohol. It should be noted however that this 'new' David Graham was still, in the eyes of many, a grim-faced, pedantic golfer on the course and a staid, humorless individual off it.

* * *

It was in 1974 that David and Maureen Graham's son, Andrew, was born. This was especially joyous since they had earlier lost premature twin boys only a few days after birth. This tragic event was sensitively reported in the local newspaper. See Appendix II.

The extra responsibility of providing security for a family now sat beside David's ever-present burning ambition to "show all my critics that they were wrong about me." It is somewhat ironic that this new sense of responsibility actually resulted in David applying less pressure on himself to succeed. He had always felt that only a string of good performances would change his bad attitude.

Now, parenthood and a different outlook, would contribute to improved performances and by 1975 he was back in the winners circle. After close to a three-year drought, Graham broke through in Australia to win the Wills Masters tournament, played that year at Victoria Golf Club in Melbourne. Yet again, his winning score was a 10-under par total of 282.

Today, if you were to visit David Graham at his home in Montana, USA, you would see, in his trophy room, a large photograph, taken in 1975, of David hoisting the Wills Masters trophy aloft. The trophy was a huge silver bowl and there, sitting inside the bowl and looking out at his beaming father is Andrew, Graham's son of just a few months. A son, a more responsible, less self-centred attitude and a winner's trophy. One could reasonably argue that there was a connection, a cause and effect relationship between these three developments.

In his acceptance speech after the trophy was presented to him Graham remembered his 'old Boss', George Naismith. "I cannot express enough appreciation for the way I felt, having you walk with me during the final 18 holes. I am sure that it went a long way towards making my victory possible."

It was on the Wednesday prior to the start of the Wills Masters that David Graham received a valuable reminder of the need for hard work. Practice rounds and the like had been called off because of heavy rain. As David sat at a table in the crowded lounge of the Victoria clubhouse, somebody walked past and commented, "Who is that idiot out on the practice range hitting golf balls?" Graham looked over in the direction of the practice tee and immediately recognized 'the idiot'. It was Gary Player. He thought to himself, "If Gary Player is out there hitting balls in the pouring rain, what am I doing sitting here in the clubhouse?"

Chapter 6

This valuable lesson provided by Gary Player brings back memories of how Jack Nicklaus described his initial encounter with Arnold Palmer.

"The first time I saw Arnold," he said recently, "was in 1954. I was 14 years old and playing in the Ohio Amateur. I came off the golf course in pouring rain, and there was one guy on the practice range hitting 9-irons about 10 feet high, taking big divots. Strong as an ox, just killing the ball. I watched him for a half hour in the rain because I was interested in his swing and how he was moving the ball, those low draws. Somebody said, 'Oh, that's our defending champion, Arnold Palmer'. He was still hitting balls when I left."

Three times major winner, Vijay Singh, is another who doesn't believe in sitting around in the clubhouse. At the 1992 Toyota World Match Play Championship, Singh said, "I work hard. I open the driving range and I close it. What is the point of going back to the hotel, having a drink and talking a load of bull?"

The single-minded, obsessive approach that David Graham developed to practice was seen by the golf writer from the *Golf Magazine*, Cameron Morfit, as "so relentless that he could be called a precursor to Vijay Singh, Nick Faldo and even to self-described 'control freak', Tiger Woods."

* * *

1976 proved to be the watershed year for David Graham. By the time he had won the Piccadilly World Match Play Championship at the Wentworth Golf Club just outside London, his yearly prize pool stood at just under $US300,000 and second only world-wide to Jack Nicklaus.

Graham's first win in 1976 came in Japan, in Nagoya, at the Chunichi Crowns Invitational. Six years earlier when he won the Yomiuri Open in Japan he collected a $US7,500 cheque and a small car. This time round the cheque was much larger, $US60,000, and the car considerably bigger as well.

In the Chunichi Crowns, his ultra-low round was on the first day. He shot a 63 and from there was never headed. Soon after winning in Nagoya, Graham finally got up enough courage to go to his banker in Florida and tell him about the pressure in his personal and golfing life imposed by a split with his former manager, Bucky Woy, several years previously.

David had parted ways with Woy about the same time another

of Woy's clients, Lee Trevino, also left the Woy stable. Immediately following their split, Woy hit both of them with law suits. To avoid a court case Trevino paid out, in his own words, "a small fortune," but one that he could definitely afford at that time. In David Graham's case the legal action did go to court where the ruling, in Woy's favour, required Graham to make regular annual payments to his former manager. The word amongst golfers was that the settlement was a '6-figure sum', an amount the Australian could ill afford to pay.

To David's great relief the bank loaned him the money he needed to complete the final instalment of the court-based order. He now had an orderly process for his borrowings and repayments and could set about concentrating properly on his golf.

When he won in Japan he knew that he still had an immediate challenge ahead of him. That was to win in the USA again. Six weeks later, at the Westchester Classic, in New York State, he did just that. As in Japan he led from 'go to whoa' and, just like in Nagoya, he pocketed a cheque for $60,000.

After winning the Westchester Classic, at that time the richest tournament on the US tour, David Graham did not have long to wait for his next US tour win. A few weeks later, he played with what one golf correspondent described as "ruthless consistency" to win the American Golf Classic. Another golf scribe labelled his rounds at Akron's Firestone Country Club (69, 67, 69 and 69) as "a cold-blooded gimlet-eyed job." David's putting in this event, and in the subsequent World Match Play title, was phenomenal. At Firestone's Old

Giving the victory sign after winning the 1976 Westchester Classic, New York.

course, noted for its very fast greens, he had only one three-putt green in 72 holes.

David's wife, Maureen, described his overall performance at Akron rather differently. "David just casually goes along and does his little thing." Her final comment revealed her husband's real ambition for the immediate future. "But all he wants now," she said, "is the Australian Open. He's really going after that."

David and Maureen Graham delighted after his victory in the 1976 World Matchplay event at Wentworth, London.

'Good guy' David hits jackpot

From BOB MacDONALD

DAVID GRAHAM... $250,000 target.

NEW YORK, Mon. — David Graham now seems certain to be the first Australian golfer to win $250,000 in a year.

That's his target before he flies home from the United States next month for the Australian Open.

And he's going after the Open, the only major Australian tournament he has never won, riding one of the hottest streaks in American golf.

His $15,000 fourth place in the World Series tournament in Akron, Ohio, yesterday, brought his earnings in seven weeks to $115,000.

It also gave him $55,000 in two weeks from the Firestone Country Club's two courses, famous as among the toughest in America.

Last week, on the new course, with 54 acres of lakes and streams, he won the $40,000 first place in the American Golf Classic.

Yesterday, on the longer north course, he was six strokes behind Jack Nicklaus in a field of 20, handpicked from the world's best golfers for 1976.

He had scored his biggest U.S. tournament win, $60,000, taking the Westchester Classic in New York in July.

His American streak followed a major tournament victory in Japan.

"Right now I'm about $230,000 for the year, which isn't bad," Graham said today. "By the time I get to Australia, hopefully that will be around quarter of a million."

He will play in only two Australian tournaments — the Open and the Westlakes Classic in Adelaide.

"I'm really looking forward to going home, playing as well as I've played this year," he said.

His last month's victories have given him new stature on the American tour.

At 30, he has already been long regarded as one of the most consistent players and "nicest blokes" on the circuit.

"You're going to be hearing a lot of him," one of America's top TV commentators told a nationwide audience last week as the cameras followed Graham up to his victory ovation on the 18th green.

"He doesn't make any funny moves when he swings. He's just a very solid player."

The same commentator reported that at the hole before a camera had toppled over, falling on a cameraman, just as Graham hit off from the tee.

"At the next green, with all the pressure of leading the tournament, he walked over to one of our crew and asked 'Is your cameraman OK?'" the commentator said.

"That's the sort of fellow he is."

Graham at the time had a four-stroke lead, but had three awesome stretches of water to cross in the last two holes.

"Everyone seemed to think I had it won, but you're never sure at Firestone where you've got blokes making sevens, eights and nines ahead of you," he said.

"The word filters through that someone has just made 10 at the 18th and it builds up the pressure.

"I think the one thing every player is more concerned about than anything else is coming into the last hole with a one or two stroke lead and making an eight..."

Bob MacDonald in The Herald *of 7 September 1976 reports on David Graham's record breaking year.*

7.

"I'LL WIN IT FOR YOU ONE DAY, BOSS."

David Graham's win in the Piccadilly World Match Play Tournament towards the end of the 1976 season made a worldwide television viewing audience sit up and, for the first time, really take notice of the slightly built Australian with the rigid upright stance and mechanical swing.

In an event that is renowned for exciting matches, David Graham featured in two classic contests. In the semi-final against Raymond Floyd he was trailing, four down after 27 holes, before surging home in 31 strokes for the last nine holes. It was sufficient to give David a victory on the final green and a place in the 36-hole final against the defending title-holder, Hale Irwin.

In the final, Graham fell behind early in the 36-hole match. He remained so for all but the final two holes of this absorbing contest. Two holes down on the 35th tee he rallied to win both the 35th and 36th holes to square the match and send it into sudden death play-off. After both players halved the first extra hole with pars, David Graham's 17-foot (5m) putt for a birdie two on the next hole sealed the victory.

That year Hale Irwin was heading for a third straight win in the World Match Play Championship, having taken the title in 1974 and 1975. Irwin felt he had outplayed the Australian in the final, but somehow, had lost the match. It was reported that Irwin was so angry with the result that, immediately after, he "kicked his golf bag right across the locker room."

The BBC television commentator, Peter Allis, summed up the final as "having been won by David Graham with a series of stupefying putts, particularly on the last half a dozen holes." His description that day of Graham's swing makes for interesting reading. "Fairly graceless in style," he noted, "Graham gives the impression, when he sets up to the ball, of a machine being aligned for action. His head is tucked into hunched-up shoulders, his legs are rather straight and the right wrist is notably arched." Allis then went on to say that even David Graham's walk is "rather on the stiff side" before concluding "but it all works very efficiently indeed."

Reviewing David Graham's outstanding 1976 year, Australian golf writer Terry Smith felt that the real strength of his game was a superlative touch with two clubs in particular, the driver and the pitching wedge. Smith also revealed a recurring nightmare of Graham's. It was one in which he leaves his favourite driver and wedge behind at an airport. He then flies off to the next tournament stop without them. In this respect Graham mirrored a similar fear of nine-times major winner, Gary Player.

Early in his career Gary Player was competing at a tournament in Japan when he came across a putter with a very distinctive blade. He tried it out and immediately felt very comfortable with it in his hands. It was old and its price just a few yen. That putter soon found a place in Player's golf bag and with it he putted his way to many victories all over the world. Whether he dreamt about it or not, Gary Player feared that somehow he would lose this putter, or that it would be stolen from his bag, "on the morning of the first round of a major."

One year, during a practice round at Augusta, Player confided to David Graham of this constant fear. In a gesture of goodwill, for which the little South African was forever grateful, David Graham 'borrowed' the putter for a few days following the Masters Tournament. During that time Graham was able to make an almost perfect replica of Player's cherished blade putter. "Just in case," he told Player, when he presented him with it at the next tournament venue.

Ever since his teenage years at Riversdale and then on the factory floor at Precision Golf Forgings in Sydney, David Graham has been fascinated by golf club design and manufacture. Bruce Devlin remembers this fascination. "In the middle of a tournament, he and I would change a full set of irons at night in the motel room, trying to improve their 'feel' for the next round. We would get those tiny cigarette lighters. About half of one gets one club head off, so five or six of them would get the whole set off."

These days there are virtually no club-makers among the professionals on the PGA tour. Even in the seventies and eighties there was only a handful who could turn their hand to club-making, and of these David Graham was certainly the most accomplished. Until he put a stop to it, players would frequently leave clubs in Graham's locker with such simple messages as, 'Please build up the grip and deliver it to me at the Greensboro Open.'

Jack Nicklaus recognised this ability soon after Graham settled in Florida. Nicklaus said of Graham, "He is the most talented club-maker in the world for his age." Not surprisingly Nicklaus went into partnership with David Graham in a club design business that proved to be very successful over more than twenty years. The most recognised of their efforts was the Jack Nicklaus Limited Edition model. Limited, quite literally, to only one thousand sets they sold out quickly. The last set went for the princely sum of US$5,400 and this more than twenty-five years ago.

By the 1990's David was consulting on golf club design for the Japanese firm, Daiwa. When Ian Baker-Finch won the 1991 British Open at Royal Birkdale he used a set of Daiwa clubs, the 273 Series designed by David Graham. The '273' had a special meaning for Graham which went back ten years earlier to 1981, but more about that 'special meaning' later.

Despite the worldwide attention that the 1976 World Match Play title afforded him, 1977 yielded, what was to David Graham, his most satisfying victory to that point. A month or two before this particular win he was successful in the South African PGA Championship. It meant that he could now claim to have won tournaments on every continent, if we exclude Antarctica. Wins in Europe, Asia, North America, South America, Australia and now Africa put him in a very select group. It also fulfilled his 1970 stated ambition "to prove I can be consistently good all over the world."

* * *

The 1977 Australian Open was scheduled for The Australian Golf Club in Sydney. The course had recently been extensively redesigned by Jack Nicklaus into a long and challenging American-style test of golf. David Graham got to Sydney early so he could acquaint himself thoroughly with the new layout. He had tried unsuccessfully to win his national

Open on numerous occasions since his debut in the Open back in 1962. Then, as a sixteen year old, he had struggled under the pressure of playing in his first big tournament. Disconsolate on his return to Riversdale he had promised George Naismith that he would "win it for you one day Boss."

On the eve of the 1977 Open it appeared that the promised 'one day' would not be that particular year. David's driver, normally very reliable, was misbehaving. His tee shots in the pro-am were so wild that he declined to put his card in. Not for the first time, Graham sought some answers on the practice range from Bruce Devlin. As darkness fell on the eve of the first round, the two of them could be seen in earnest discussion between each of Graham's practice shots. To make matters worse, Graham was suffering badly from bronchitis and, later that same evening, it was discovered he was bleeding from his right ear due to pressure built up by the congestion in his head.

The field that year was one of the best to ever contest the Stonehaven Cup. As well as the best players from Australia, more than thirty US tour regulars had made the trip down under. They included such major winners as Jack Nicklaus, Ray Floyd, Hubert Green and Jerry Pate. David Graham's health issues and indifferent pre-tournament form were expected by many to see him finish well down the final scoreboard.

On a windy first day Graham still struggled for consistency with his driver but some excellent short game play meant that his round of 74 was only four strokes worse than the day's best score.

In the second round the wind was much stronger and frequent rain showers, complete with lightning, made scoring even more difficult. Because the competitors were using the larger American ball, to satisfy a major sponsor of the Open, several tee markers were moved forward to compensate for the strong wind gusts. In these terrible conditions David's 71 kept him in the top dozen players at the halfway point.

Conditions on the Saturday were only marginally better, but David Graham's swing was now much more in tune, especially when compared to where it was in the days leading up to the Open. He went round in 68, the best score of anyone in the third round.

Graham teed off in the last group on Sunday. His playing partner, the American, Don January, led the Championship, and David Graham

Chapter 7

*Holding the Stonehaven Cup after winning the
1977 Australian Open at the Australian GC in Sydney.*

by one stroke. Throughout the first fifteen holes they traded shot for shot. The soft American-type sand that Nicklaus had put into the bunkers during his rebuilding of the course claimed Graham on the 13th and 16th holes where, on both occasions, his ball buried in a green side bunker. By getting up and down to save two pars on these crucial holes he kept in front of January. Then, on the seventeenth hole, his birdie from 12 feet (4m), gave him a cushion of several strokes heading down the par five eighteenth hole. Walking up to the last green, after a third shot to the heart of the green and with victory assured, David

After winning the 1977 Australian Open, he and Jack Nicklaus compare trophies. Photo courtesy Australian Golf Magazine.

Graham acknowledged the cheers of the huge crowd on the embankment overlooking the green. Two putts later he signed for a 71 and a three-stroke triumph.

Peter Thomson, writing in the Melbourne newspaper *The Herald* the next day, said that "David Graham played with determination and poise, refusing to allow his poorer shots to upset him. It looked as if he knew right from the start of the final round he was destined to win. Time and again stout-hearted putting saved him."

David spoke to George Naismith by telephone in the hour after the presentation and arranged for Naismith to fly up to Sydney the next day. The photograph of their reunion on the Monday captures the joy and pride shared by both in the events of the previous few days.

There was a nice symmetry to Graham's win and the win forty years earlier by a young George Naismith in the 1937 Australian Open.

Both Opens were played at The Australian Golf Club in the Sydney suburb of Kensington. The winds were up during the week of the Open in 1937 and again in 1977. If anything the wind was stronger in 1937 as only twice in 460 completed rounds was a score lower than 71 returned. Graham and Naismith were good wind players. Both players had very strong wrists and relatively short, controlled back swings, ideal for punching golf shots into and under the wind.

*Re-united with mentor George Naismith after winning the
1977 Australian Open at The Australian GC in Sydney.
Photo courtesy* The Herald & Weekly Times.

The following year, 1978, produced just one win, the Mexico Cup but throughout that year and into 1979, David Graham continued to fine tune his swing and, more importantly, undertake what he later described as "mental toughness training for golf."

* * *

Like all professional golfers, David Graham was always on the lookout for that perfect wedge. Over the years this search led to a large collection of wedges of different specifications and by a variety of club manufacturers. When Tom Watson chipped out of the rough at Pebble Beach and into the cup on the seventy-first hole of the 1982 US Open, he broke out of a tie with Jack Nicklaus and went on to win. The Wilson wedge he used that day had, several months earlier, been picked out of David Graham's collection, where according to Watson, "he had more than twenty lined up in his garage."

A lighter moment with good friend and competitor, Jack Nicklaus, at the 1977 Australian Open. Photo courtesy Australian Golf Magazine.

8.

"AT THE APEX OF HIS CAREER HE WAS ABOUT AS CONVIVIAL AS A TRAPPIST MONK."

Prior to the 1979 PGA Championship at Oakland Hills, Michigan, David Graham was not particularly happy with his golf game. He was winless through the first half of 1979 and his only victory in 1978 had come in the somewhat obscure Mexico Cup. His last victory on the PGA tour was back in 1976 at the American Golf Classic. But he felt that a tip from Gary Player late in 1978 would help take his game to the next level.

Ever since he started playing golf as a professional, Graham had swung with a three-quarter backswing. He just wasn't comfortable taking the club back to parallel. Player's advice to Graham was to stretch out his backswing and, to help feeling comfortable about it, practise with a weighted driver. Envious of the Jack Nicklaus long backswing during practice rounds in Florida, he once asked Jack why he had such a wide shoulder turn and therefore a long backswing. Evidently Nicklaus thought about this for a little while before answering, "Good shots are worth waiting for."

Back in his workshop he found a persimmon-headed driver into which he drilled several big holes. Next he poured molten lead into the holes and also down the shaft of the club. After it all cooled down he put a new grip on it. "I liked it so much", he said, "that I took to actually hitting balls with it." It did the trick and in the summer of 1979 he swung his woods and irons "back to parallel for the first time and started to play really well."

The Oakland Hills course near Detroit, Michigan, had long been dubbed 'the monster' and its extreme length of 7,014 yards (6376m) was expected to again test the best golfers on Tour. It had been well watered so little roll on drives was likely. Also, its elevated greens and numerous double-deck bunkers were thought to make par for 4 rounds close to a winning score on the Donald Ross designed course.

After 3 rounds David Graham was several shots back, but with only a handful of golfers ahead of him. Although not out of it, he knew it would take a round that was in the sixties (par was 72) for him to have any chance. The fact that he carded a seven under score of 65 to tie Ben Crenshaw at 272 is not even half the story of that remarkable last day at Oakland Hills.

The real story of the 1979 US PGA Championship is contained in just four holes, the first of which was the seventy-second hole, the last of regulation play. With Graham standing on the last tee, two strokes ahead of his nearest competitor, it did appear that this hole would indeed be the final one of the Championship.

David Graham had found the fairway virtually every time during this fourth round but, for whatever reason, pressure or a backswing to less than parallel perhaps, he pushed his tee shot on eighteen a long way to the right. At the press conference later he would say, "When I started my backswing, I woke up to what was really going on out there. It was my worst drive for the week." Writing in *Golf Monthly*, Joe Doan considered, "What may have led to Graham's collapse on the final hole is that he was taunted by a handful of spectators on the eighteenth tee, and was also irritated by photographers who had swarmed in to film his triumphal walk down the last fairway."

David Graham's experience with a partisan American gallery, during that final round, was a precursor of fellow Australian, Craig Parry's, similar fate at the 1992 US Masters Tournament. Throughout Parry's last eighteen holes, a very vocal gallery was keen for 'their man', Fred Couples, to come home with a victory. Parry in contention to win himself, let the Couples supporters get to him, and he fell by the wayside. People were continually coughing during his swing and someone even pushed over a chair just as he was about to putt. "I three-putted three holes in a row", he said later, "and the crowd cheered every time. I've never seen anything so one-sided!"

The spectators were taunting David Graham about his disposition. Playing brilliantly and with the Championship seemingly in his grasp, they wanted more emotion from the Australian. Graham, however, was as grimfaced and resolute of jaw, as he had been all afternoon.

The following is a description of Ben Hogan, written in 1965 by the American writer, Alfred Wright, but it could also have been penned to describe David Graham in 1979. "At the apex of his career, he (Hogan) was about as convivial as a Trappist monk. He conquered golf with willpower, forcing his slight physique to its utmost."

Some time before the 1979 PGA Championship, David Graham had been asked by a journalist why he was so dour on the golf course, even when things were going well for him. His reply is particularly interesting given what transpired on the 72nd hole at Oakland Hills.

"I am too scared to be a showman", he told the journalist. "I could never punch the air with my fist (say) because in the back of my mind I was aware that I could double-bogey the last hole and bring about the most embarrassing situation of my life."

The errant drive on Oakland Hills' eighteenth went so far right it landed in a relatively clear spot. Graham had an open shot to the green but being so wide and with so many people milling about he couldn't work out his yardage from an eighteenth fairway sprinkler head. Back then a lot of young players, Graham included, were copying the Jack Nicklaus method of doing his own yardages and club selection. It became a sort of status thing 'to play like Jack did'. David's caddy that year was Willie Peterson, but Graham was making all his own decisions concerning yardages, clubs, reading putts, etc. Twenty years after the event, when asked about his second shot to eighteen, he revealed this brief conservation with Peterson.

"When I couldn't find the yardage I said to Willie, how far is it? Well, Willie's reply stunned me." He said, "You haven't asked me one question all the way around. I don't know. Figure it out yourself." Visibly upset Graham fumbled around and finally hit a 6-iron. It was on line with the flag but, probably because it was one club too many, flew over the green. He chilli-dipped his first chip shot, which didn't even make it to the green, and then over-hit the next chip, five feet past the hole. He still had a shortish putt to win the title and everything that went with it. He missed and sudden death was now the reality.

The Championship was still there to be won but what was gone with that double-bogey six were two cheques of US$50,000 each. A golf magazine had put up a US$50,000 bonus for a four-round championship record and a further US$50,000 for someone to break the single round PGA record of 63, held incidentally by a fellow Australian, Bruce Crampton. Whether David was aware on the 72nd tee that a par four would earn him $50,000 and a birdie-three $100,000 is not clear. But if he was, it certainly wouldn't have lessened any pressure he was already feeling.

In contrast to Graham's account of his conversation with Peterson half-way down the 72nd fairway, Peterson told John Ingham, an English golf writer, that he'd told Graham to play for the centre of the green "but no, he had to go for the flagstick, positioned wickedly." Perhaps David Graham did calculate the monetary riches that a birdie would bring. What is not in dispute is Willie's remark to David as they walked up to the scorer's tent and David's abrupt reply. "Don't worry, Boss, we'll get 'em in the play off." To which Graham said, "Don't even speak to me. The further you stay away from me, the happier I'll be. Just carry the clubs."

David Graham's state of mind, as he signed for a round of 65, was not improved by the PGA officials hurrying him off to the first play-off hole. They were concerned that there would not be enough daylight to conclude the Championship that evening (and so upset American television heads) if the play-off went longer than one or two holes.

So to the play-off, and one of the most dramatic in Major history. The first two tee shots would possibly have reminded David of the 1977 Australian Open play-off with Peter Thomson. Crenshaw hit a beautiful drive smack down the middle of the fairway (just like Thomson in 1977) and David (as in 1977) hit a flat duck hook.

When he reached his ball all David could do was chip it on to the fairway some 100 yards (90m) short of the green. He watched Crenshaw hit a good second shot to about 30 feet from the hole. David's "not so good" wedge to the green left him a few feet inside Crenshaw. When Crenshaw narrowly missed his birdie Graham had to hole out from 25 feet (9m), downhill across the green, to stay alive. He would say later, "I think God blessed me that day, that's the only thing I can think of, because somehow, still in a daze, I made the putt."

The next hole was virtually a repeat of the first. A shortish par 5 it was reached by Ben in two strokes but David's second went into the gallery packed around the green. Crenshaw's eagle attempt slid by and

Chapter 8

On the road to victory in the 1979 US PGA Championship at Oakland Hills CC, Michigan.

David Graham: From Ridicule to Acclaim

AAP-AP satellite picture

David Graham flourishes his putter after winning the US PGA championship sudden-death playoff on Sunday.

BIRMINGHAM, Michigan, Monday.—David Graham stood on the 18th tee of Oakland Hills course yesterday needing only a par four to win the US Professional Golfers' Association championship with a record low total.

"When I started my backswing, I woke up to what was really going on out there," he said later. "I hit a really dreadful drive, my worst this week."

Unnerved, Graham hit his drive out to the left, missed the green with a six-iron approach, fluffed the pitch shot, put the next just over a metre past the hole, missed the putt, then sank the next for a double-bogey six.

He finished with an eight-under-par 272 to tie with Ben Crenshaw.

Graham had started the round well. "I knew I had to make a lot of birdies," he said later. And he did—seven, plus the one that won him the title in the playoff.

He looked a beaten man when faced with an eight-metre putt at the first playoff hole to stay alive, but sank it. He sank a two-metre putt at the second to tie again, then a three-metre putt at the next for a birdie to beat Crenshaw, who bunkered his tee shot.

Graham took first prize money of $53,000. But had he broken the four-round PGA record of 271, he would have won another $44,000, and a birdie for a one-round record of 62 would have won another $44,000.

Earlier this season, Graham, 33, had had such a bad start to the season that "I even thought it was time I went into golf club designing full time."

AAP-Reuter

Match report in sport, back page.

Newspaper report (courtesy Sydney Morning Herald) the day after winning the US PGA title at Oakland Hills.

Graham was again left with a must-hole putt of 10 feet (3m), but again down the slope. Again he holed it.

The third and final play-off hole was almost an anti-climax, but there was more drama on the tee of the 204 yard (185m) par three hole. As David stepped up to hit his favourite 4-iron he had to back away twice. The first time it was due to a young child falling out of a nearby elm tree. The second time was when a television crane let out a loud diesel roar, followed by a marshal bellowing almost as loudly, "Turn that thing off." Seemingly back in control of his emotions Graham then struck his 4-iron to 6 feet (2m)

Phil Tressider reports in Sydney's Daily Telegraph of 5 August 1979.

from the pin. He described it as his second best strike of the day, the best coming at the 15th where the same club from 190 yards (173m) finished just two inches (5cm) from the cup for a birdie that gave him a vital two stroke lead with three holes to play. David again holed the putt but it didn't matter so much this time as Ben, who had been bunkered off the tee, had already hit his par putt from 15 feet well past the hole.

* * *

There are quite a few interesting postscripts from the 1979 US PGA and, in particular, the events of the last four holes. Ben Crenshaw had finished runner-up in no less than three of the last four tournaments he had entered prior to this event, one of them being the 1979 British Open. Understandably he complained after his sudden death defeat,

David Graham with the trophy at the Oakland Hills Country Club in Michigan after becoming the first Australian to win the US PGA championship since Jim Ferrier in 1947.

"I hate second." Crenshaw in fact has one of the worst sudden death play-off records on the PGA Tour, losing his first six before finally winning one. In his press conference in 1979 he summed up what had just happened out on the course as accurately and concisely as any journalist there. "I shouldn't have been in the play-off, but once there I shouldn't have lost."

He then went on to point out that people have no concept of how tough it is to have a tournament, especially a big one, wrapped up as Graham did, and then let it get away on the very last hole. "It's excruciating," he said, "It tears a man to pieces. You just don't realise how hard it is to then have to come out for a play-off."

Thirty years after Crenshaw's loss another American golfer went into a play-off for a major championship in somewhat similar circumstances. The golfer was Kenny Perry and the major was the 2009 US Masters.

This time it was Perry who made a mess of the last two holes just when, like Graham in 1979, he seemed to have the Championship securely in his grasp. Bogeys on holes 17 and 18 saw Perry slip back into a three-man play-off with Chad Campbell and the big-hitting Argentinean, Angel Cabrera. When Cabrera parred the second extra hole to Perry's bogey it was Cabrera's Championship, Campbell having been eliminated on the first play-off hole.

A comment from the disappointed Perry, made during his press conference, has relevance for Cabrera and David Graham, both two-time major championship winners. Angel Cabrera had previously won the 2004 US Open. Reflecting on the dramatic conclusion to the 2009 Masters, Perry said, "Only the great players get it done, the average players don't."

Michael McDonnell, a golf correspondent for over thirty years with London's *Daily Mail*, put it this way. "The blinding truth about losing is that for all the hard luck, bad bounces, poor lies and other mitigating factors that may have come into play, the other guy played better when it really mattered. It is that gruesome realisation that makes the journey home so hard to bear." David Graham, by his own admission, was in that 'excruciating' position. "Oh, I was an accident looking for a place to happen," he said later.

In the euphoria of the win, immediately after sinking his putt on the third play-off hole, one thing was noticeable. It is usual for caddies to run across and embrace their player with much outward display of emotion. At Oakland Hills on that late Sunday afternoon there was a noticeable apprehension from David Graham before he put his arms somewhat hesitatingly around Willie Peterson.

* * *

In retirement, more than thirty years after the US PGA Championship, David Graham still sees that particular victory as his most significant in a long career. The PGA Tour in those days was not a fully exempt tour, as it is now. Only the top sixty players were sure of a spot each week. But the PGA win carried with it a ten-year exemption and according to Graham "secured my life." It confirmed to him and his wife Maureen that coming to America was "the best decision we ever made." For the first time Graham had the freedom to pick and choose where and when he could play. It cut out the need for Monday pre-qualifying even if, over the next decade, he did happen to slip out of the top sixty money winners on Tour.

Talking on Melbourne radio in December 2006, Graham attributed the 1979 win with even more importance. "Without it I may never have won again, certainly not a major championship like a US Open. Losing that PGA after the double-bogey on the 72nd hole would have changed everything, for the worst. Things like that ruin people's careers. Look at that Van de Velde guy (at the 2005 British Open). I was able to stay in the US, buy houses and put the kids in good schools. I feel very blessed."

David Graham was full of praise for the runner up in 1979, Ben Crenshaw. "Fortunately," he said in 2011, "I never experienced losing a play-off in one of the four major championships, but I know it takes a very strong person to overcome something like that. Many players have not been able to do that, but Ben Crenshaw was an exception. He went on to have a great career and is a two-time US Masters Champion. I take my hat off to him."

Finally, the thoughts of two people on opposite sides of the world in the immediate aftermath of Graham's first win in a major. When David got back to his Florida home a few days later there was a telegram waiting for him that said, "You showed what you are made of in the first two holes of the play-off. I'm proud of you." It was from Jack Nicklaus.

In the Melbourne suburb of Burwood, and in the hour after her son's final putt was holed, David's mother found a quiet corner and "cried my eyes out, with pride and with joy, yes, but more from the release of all that tension that had built up over four days." She had often thought of how she might react to such a momentous win. "I pictured the champagne flowing and cheers so loud they could be heard a mile away, but it was all so different to what I thought it would be."

Chapter 8

After sinking a long putt from off the green during the 1980 Australian Open at the Lakes GC in Sydney. The arrow is pointing at his airborne putter. Photo courtesy Australian Golf Magazine.

9.

"ANYBODY CAN GET LUCKY AND WIN A MAJOR CHAMPIONSHIP ONCE. IT TAKES A GREAT PLAYER TO WIN TWO."

Returning to Australia for the 1979 summer golf season David Graham showed some of his major-winning form to local galleries. He captured the West Lakes Classic in South Australia and, soon after, the Air New Zealand Open.

The next major championship in golf after the US PGA is always the following year's US Masters tournament. In 1980 David Graham made his regular trip to Augusta in the week before the tournament started. For quite a few years, Jack Nicklaus had invited Graham to accompany him on this pre-tournament preparation week. In this particular week Graham's practice form was excellent and he had high hopes for another top performance in a major.

The opening round was played in a brisk wind but it didn't prevent Graham from carding a 66. The next morning the golf correspondent for London's *The Times* newspaper wrote, "With a player of Graham's ruthless accuracy, it is almost a question of just counting the putts to get his 18 hole score."

The exciting young Spanish golfer, Severiano Ballesteros, playing later in the day, matched Graham's 66. The day was notable for one other score. Tom Weiskopf hit no less than five balls into Rae's Creek at the short par three 12th to eventually set a US Masters record high score of 13 on one hole.

In the second round Graham had to 'count' considerably more putts than the previous day. Yet, his 73 was still good enough for second place although he was now four strokes behind Ballesteros. On this day,

Weiskopf only hit two balls into the water at the 12th, so his 7 there was a full 6 strokes better than in the first round.

Saturday's 'moving day' saw Ballesteros race ahead of his nearest opponent. A superb 68 had him in the lead by 7 strokes with one round to play. David Graham was still in second place but now equal with two others.

As Ballesteros started to stumble on the final day it was not David Graham but another Australian golfer who challenged the Spaniard. Jack Newton was "holing everything" on the glassy Augusta greens and drew within a couple of shots of Ballesteros midway through the back nine. Ballesteros steadied over the last 4 holes and ran out the winner by 3 strokes. Newton was equal second whilst Graham slipped to fifth despite a solid final round of 70. It was to be the closest he ever came to wearing a green jacket in more than a dozen attempts at Augusta.

From there it was down to South America for another victory, the Heublin Classic in Brazil. Back in the United States he teamed up with fellow Aussie, Jan Stephenson, to win a different type of tournament, the World Mixed Teams Championship. To cap off another terrific year he raced away with the Mexican Open, shooting a 62 and a 64 in his 72 hole

With his cheque for $13,000 after winning the 1979 West Lakes Classic in Adelaide. Photo courtesy Australian Golf Magazine.

winning total of 20 under par 264. His winning margin of 8 strokes, over runner-up Jerry Pate, was, and remains, his biggest winning margin in a professional tournament.

In November 1980 he played an 18-hole match against Hale Irwin at Oatlands Golf Club in Sydney. It was one of many played around the world for television as part of "The World Series of Golf" sponsored by European ferry operators, Townsend-Thoresen. Naturally, it created considerable interest among the club members and local golfers who attended in droves.

It was unusually hot for late spring and the greens were left uncut that day to prevent them from being burnt off by the sun. Walking off the 2nd green, David Graham loudly remarked, "These greens are like carpet – shag pile carpet". This visibly upset the greenkeeper, a number of his staff and others who were within earshot.

The 11th hole at Oatlands is a par 5 of 518 yards (471m) with a slight dog-leg left and a small lake covering the left half of the fairway about 300 yards (270m) from the tee. Graham pushed his drive into trees on the right, chose a two-iron and played a magnificent shot through a narrow opening with a slight fade to perfect position just short of the green.

One of the older Oatlands members watched in jaw-dropping admiration and said to David, "You know, I would have just chipped it on to the fairway." David Graham curtly replied, "That's why I'm playing and you're watching."

* * *

His excellent form continued into 1981 and after several high finishes on the tour he won in the desert at the Phoenix Open, Arizona. Again he proved to be a final round specialist. A birdie on the 72nd hole in a closing 66 snatched a one shot victory from Lon Hinkle.

Another good display on the hilly fairways and rolling greens at Augusta in the 1981 US Masters saw Graham in good shape for that year's next major, the US Open.

The choice of Merion Golf Club for major events always represents a particular type of challenge for professional golfers. Short, by US Open standards, the club's East Course at Ardmore, Pennsylvania, had, nevertheless, destroyed many famous golfers' cards since it was first used for a US Open in 1934.

A month before the 1981 US Open, David Graham's health was deteriorating. He lacked his usual energy, felt weak and was tired all the time. He told his doctor in Dallas, "I can sleep ten hours and still wake up tired." Extensive testing allayed the initial fears of heart trouble. The medical opinion was that his system lacked potassium. Since arriving in America in 1969, Graham had not only worked hard on his physical strength and flexibility, but also watched his health very carefully. To supplement his diet, he did what many golfers who travel all over the world do, he took up to twenty vitamin pills each day.

The recommendation now was for him to build up his potassium levels by eating a lot more fruit, especially bananas, and green vegetables. Eggs and meat were out, at least for a few weeks.

It worked, and able to practise in earnest again, his form quickly returned to its early season standard. In a practice round at Merion, playing partner, Gary Player, remarked, "David, I'm damned if I know why you haven't won more major tournaments."

In the first two rounds David Graham's accurate and consistent iron play found many greens in regulation where his confident putting produced two excellent scores of 68. A steady par round of 70 on Saturday saw him well placed, three strokes behind the 54-hole leader, George Burns.

As was the case two years previously, at Oakland Hills, the story of this major was Sunday's final round. Burns and Graham were paired for the final round and presented a stark contrast as they walked off the first tee. The slightly built Australian was towered over by the 6 feet 5 inch (196cm) Burns. Burns had a wide flowing swing from his somewhat stooped stance. David Graham on the other hand was much more erect and his swing, as always, rather mechanical looking.

Early in the final round, George Burns started to hit his drivers left finding the thickish rough on several holes. David Graham was finding every fairway and almost every green and by the 14th hole had drawn level with Burns. With the only other contenders, Rogers, Nicklaus and Crenshaw falling away, it was down to Burns and Graham to fight it out over the concluding five holes.

On the 14th hole, a 414 yard (376m) par four and one of the most difficult on the course, Graham hit probably the best shot of the final day. A soaring 7-iron to a tiny target area on the green stopped six feet from the hole. A birdie there, and another on the next hole, where his 8-iron second shot finished next to the pin, took him to a two stroke lead. Although Burns chipped in at the short 17th for a birdie, Graham had his measure. Two superb pressure shots on the 18th and two putts from 18 feet sealed Graham's second major title, this time by a more comfortable three strokes. As Walter Hagen had observed many years earlier, "Anybody can get lucky and win a major championship once. It takes a great player to win two."

In an interview for a golf magazine in 1999, David Graham singled out his win in the 1981 US Open as being "far more sentimental" than his win in the 1979 PGA Championship. "When you win a national open you really do become part of the history of the game." This explains the tearful hug for wife Maureen as soon as he left the 18th green and the emotional meeting that followed with his very good mate, Bruce Devlin, in the Merion Golf Club locker room.

Winning at Merion had special significance for David Graham. It was a very traditional style of golf course and the Club was steeped in golfing lore. Also, previous Open winners there included golfing legends, Ben Hogan and Lee Trevino. For Graham's part, "being the first Australian to win a US Open and doing it at Merion, which is put in the same category as an Open win at Pebble Beach and stuff like that, made it all the more memorable."

There had been lower rounds played in the US Open but few, if any, drew the type of accolades that David Graham received for that final 18 holes. If we give him the benefit of the six inches (15cm) by which his ball ran off the first fairway and the two times his approach shot to a green was fractionally off the putting surface but on the fringe (from where he putted both times) he played flawless golf from tee to green. It made sense. One of golf's most exacting course set-ups being tamed by one of its most exacting players.

The doyen of American golf writers, Herbert Warren Wind, wrote the next day, "It has been a long time since we last saw a golfer play such brilliant, forceful, technically pure shots on the final holes of the Open.

Burns did not lose the championship. Graham had the courage to try to win it, and he did so by hitting the kind of iron shots that one expects from Ben Hogan. They were struck decisively, they travelled in the right trajectory, they covered the flag, and they pulled up abruptly when they touched down on the green. It was a genuinely memorable performance."

* * *

Back home in Dallas, Ben Hogan himself phoned Graham to offer his congratulations for "one of the best rounds of golf I have ever seen." Amongst the numerous calls he received from his peers was the one his wife Maureen took at home whilst David was "off somewhere." It was from Tom Weiskopf.

During those days many of the professionals used to tinker with their clubs all the time and always searching for that perfect one. Lee Trevino quickly identified Graham as a perfectionist. "David" he said, "is the only guy I've seen who re-gripped his clubs every day before he practised. He'd come out with a pair of scissors and a roll of tape and lighter fluid and put new grips on, let them dry for five minutes, and then he'd hit balls. He had all the grass on the practice range dead from lighter fluid." This search for perfection was especially true of David Graham and Tom Weiskopf. The two of them would often drive around to old golf shops and the like "looking for that magical driver and stuff like that." When Weiskopf called the Graham house he told Maureen "Whatever clubs David used at Merion, tell him never to fiddle with them again."

Graham never did alter those clubs in any way. He has them to this very day, along with a collection of golf clubs that, at one stage, exceeded 4,000 in total. One other thing that he didn't change during that last round 67 was his golf ball.

Golf balls in the 1970's were a different species from those of today. They had liquid centres that were very vulnerable to heat. Players would never leave them in the trunk of a car for any length of time, or in a locker room that was not air-conditioned. There was also much greater variation in quality from one ball to another. David Graham used the same ball from the opening tee shot to the final putt "because that ball just felt perfect for me."

Chapter 9

Hugged by his caddy after winning the 1981 US Open at Merion GC in Ardmore, Pennsylvania.

On the Wednesday after Graham's US Open triumph, the golf writer for Melbourne newspaper *The Herald,* Jack Dillon, interviewed 'the proudest man in Australia at present'. It was of course David's old mentor, George Naismith. George told Dillon, "You might not believe it, but I predicted that David would win the US title one day. I told him this when he was a youngster and just starting out."

George, who no longer played golf because of a debilitating back injury, watched every second of the Open telecast but, like every other viewer in the country, was dismayed when his picture blacked out just as 'his boy' was walking on to the 18th green to putt out for the title.

What did David Graham himself remember most about that closing 67 at Merion? The simple answer to this question is "not very much." Memorable it may well have been for those who witnessed it that warm June day either at the course or on television, but for the man himself it remains "a bit of a blur." In fact the only really clear memory he has is a bad one, his three putts at the fifth hole.

Not long after Graham finished his round he was surprised to hear people telling him the details (fairways and greens hit in regulation) of how well he had played. "I had no idea. I only vaguely recall talking with my caddie coming up 18 and the two shots and two putts I had on that final hole."

Writing in 2006 in *Golf Digest* magazine he admitted that, "It's a good thing they have a video tape of it. It is only by looking at film of the Open that I can see where the flagsticks were located on the greens and my shots into them." On a day when he probably should remember everything, David Graham has always had trouble "reconstructing what happened from the first tee on," and in turn, has been intrigued by this short-term memory loss ever since.

In his book "Mental Toughness Training for Golf", written in 1988, he looked back at that day and feels that his lack of detailed recall of "what happened" was because he had entered what is called 'the zone'. He describes 'the zone' as "a state of mind close to being hypnotised, where everything takes on a dreamy, tranquil quality." Tony Jacklin once described this state of mind as "getting into an atmosphere and there's magic there." "If things were going well, I was alive," he said, "like an electric light bulb shining in the middle of the fairway and everything (I wanted) was going to happen."

Unlike the closing stages of most big tournaments, Graham claimed that on this particular day he was "virtually oblivious to the tremendous pressure I was under." Unusually, for him, he was not fussing over the technical aspects of his swing and "was almost completely unaware of the thousands of people in the gallery, the television cameras and even the closest competitors making a run to overtake me."

When playing the last round of the 1986 US Open at Shinnecock Hills the eventual winner, Raymond Floyd, walked off the 10th green, looked directly at his wife but in his own words, "didn't see her, I was so focused."

"That day, it felt like I was playing in slow motion," Floyd said. "I could see the future. I knew what my shots would do before I hit them. It was like someone else was playing, and I was just watching him. And I had 'the stare' that goes with intense focus. I can't induce it. It's there or it's not. But when I was in the hunt, and I had 'the stare', I never lost once."

The 2010 Greenbrier Classic golf tournament played in West Virginia, USA, was won by Australia's Stuart Appleby. In the last round Appleby fired an 11 under par, 59. After this amazing round of golf, Stuart figured that he too had visited that elusive state of mind, 'the zone'. As the final round got underway, Stuart and his caddy were aware of Appleby's "level of calm, focused intensity." As birdie putt after birdie putt dropped into the cup, Stuart became "excited at the potential for the future. I was definitely excited but, strangely, not daunted by the occasion or the prospect. So what is the zone? I think it exists on those rare occasions when there is an absence of concern over the result, of a particular shot or a key putt."

Like all golfers who have experienced this mental and physical 'automatic pilot' David Graham tried his utmost to recapture it. And like all of those golfers it proved to be an elusive and frustrating pursuit.

* * *

One of David Graham's more permanent memories of Merion will surely be, not from 1981, but from twenty-five years later in 2006. That was the year Merion Cricket Club, as it was originally named, celebrated the opening of their club back in 1906, some six years before the golf course was built on the site. As a band played the Club had Graham go back down the fairway to the 18th tee. From there he walked down the steep slope from the tee to the fairway before coming into sight over the crest of the hill that is some two hundred yards (180m) from the green. As he appeared the members, who had gathered all around the 18th green, gave him "the most wonderful applause," all the way up to the green. As he said "It was like coming home, really."

10.

"MAKING HAY WHILE THE SUN SHINES."

In the two months after winning the US Open, David Graham experienced what every US Open winner has to go through – a whirlpool of media, sponsor and public attention that places inordinate demands on a player's time. For David Graham it was particularly difficult to handle. "To go from being a very private person myself to having to be extremely public, severely affected my frame of mind" he said when back in Australia the following year.

Graham's performances in the remaining Tour events of 1981 were nothing to write home about. Fortunately an escape from the pressures in the United States came in the form of an invitation to play in the Lancome Trophy. Held every year towards the end of the European season, it was a favourite of many American based golfers as well. Played at a picturesque parkland course just outside Paris, it proved to be the tonic David Graham needed at that time. Taking Maureen with him, they "went out shopping and to some lovely restaurants, went for long walks after dinner" and he genuinely relaxed for the first whole week since Merion. The net result was that he was able to go to the golf course "ready to give those six or seven hours of concentration needed to play well over the few days of the tournament." Play well he did, winning the Trophy by two shots with yet another sub-70 score in the final round. Although the next year, 1982, was to be a lean one, so far as victories were concerned, it was in Paris twelve months later, that he won his second Lancome Trophy. It was his only tournament win for that year.

1982 may have yielded just the one victory but it reaped rich rewards for the Australian in other ways. In the space of an eleven week journey through nine countries, the reigning US Open Champion picked up more than $US300,000 in appearance money and endorsements.

Speaking in January 1982, at the start of this lucrative journey, he was realistic about cashing in on his US Open title.

"Right now people are pouring offers at me. But it is only temporary, as long as I am the champion. Come June 1982, there is, in all likelihood, going to be a new US Open Champion. Sponsors are going to want him, not the '81 winner. I've got to make hay while the sun shines."

David Graham's regular summer sojourn in Australia was expected to be, in late 1981, a triumphant homecoming for him. It turned out to be something else.

There were problems almost from the outset. He missed the cut in the West Lakes Classic and came to Sydney for the NSW Open with his usually deadly driving accuracy gone and much of the rest of his game on the missing list as well. Once again he had to face the ignominy of missing the cut. In the press tent, minutes after his second round, it was obvious his two successive failures had deeply disturbed him.

Several causes were offered by Graham in an interview that was more of an introspective psychoanalysis than the usual post-round discussion of birdies and bogeys. He blamed an inability to relax, the enormous demands on his time and the fact that he was missing his wife and two sons. If there was to be one main factor in his poor displays it was, he emphasised, the fact that he was trying too hard to do well. He felt that he had been trying probably harder than at any other time, to win on home soil. What did impress the assembled journalists was David Graham's willingness to discuss his poor form in a frank and honest way. The David Graham of some years earlier might well have stormed away from the course and spoken to nobody. So often branded as dour and humourless, he got a laugh out of everyone there when he compared his two missed cuts with that win at Merion.

"I was overwhelmed by the reaction back here in Australia to my win. I got all the papers with the front-page stuff. Unbelievable, really, I'm on page one again, but this time it's because I'm shooting 78s. A few months ago I went to the White House and met the President. But if I can't turn this around I'll be just another face in the crowd."

* * *

Chapter 10

Appearance money paid to high profile overseas golfers to come to Australia and play in Australian tournaments had long been a topic of considerable debate, especially among the locally based professionals who saw the practice as demeaning to them and the tournaments. In late 1981 this appearance money was paid, or at least a large percentage of it, to two players, Bill Rogers, the reigning British Open Champion, and David Graham, the reigning US Open Champion.

Bill Rogers lived up to his reputation as one of the very best golfers in the world at this time by winning the Australian Open in 1981, beating Greg Norman at Victoria Golf Club in Melbourne. David Graham's performances, however, stoked the fires of the appearance money debate in no uncertain manner.

David Graham felt that he had to defend the big money paid to him even though it appeared he didn't deserve it given his poor form on this trip. Quickly on to the front foot, he pulled no punches in his defence of appearance money payments.

"The PGA here doesn't have a lot of strength mainly because it doesn't have a lot of the top players. It can't be too dogmatic because it doesn't have the players. The sponsor can't justify being involved unless he has players, you know, like myself, who occasionally shoot four bad rounds but still get to go to the press tent and produce a lot of ink. I can get more ink for a sponsor by playing badly than some young player can by playing the best golf of his career. That's why we're going to have to continue importing players."

He elaborated further, "The Australian PGA is saying that instead of playing for AU$80,000 this week, we could be playing for AU$130,000 if David Graham and Bill Rogers weren't here. But if you take David Graham and Bill Rogers out, the sponsor wants to know just who will be playing for all his lovely money. It's nice to have the top Australian pros, but he wants a couple of world stars. Sponsors have brought players out in some cases, paid them money, and not been able to justify it. But if you're talking major championship winners, or of a Nicklaus or a Johnny Miller, then I think we're going to have to continue to pay them because we're at such a big geographical disadvantage. Even if we had five or six AU$200,000 tournaments, the world's best players are not going to come down to Australia to play at their own expense when they have got forty AU$350,000 tournaments right on their doorstep."

David Graham: From Ridicule to Acclaim

EXCLUSIVE INTERVIEW WITH GOLFER DAVID GRAHAM

At last the dream

Years of sacrifice and hard work paid off when Australian golfer David Graham triumphed in the historic US Open

Welcoming yellow ribbons, tied around the trees by proud neighbours, flutter outside David and Maureen Graham's roomy, ranch-style home in Dallas, Texas, US.

An enormous bowl of gift-wrapped red roses, sent in celebration by David Graham to his wife, stands just inside the front door.

And a large crate containing the treasured silver trophy for the winner of the US Open tournament lies unopened in the hallway. It has just arrived.

While Maureen Graham shows me to the living-room, David pads anxiously around in his old gardening shoes and shorts searching for a hacksaw and muttering something about not having the combination to the lock on the crate. If there is one thing he wants more than anything in the world right now, it is to open that crate.

David Graham is the first Australian to win the historic US Open. But the trophy is more than just a handsome silver prize. It represents the fulfilment of the boyhood dreams that David worked long and hard to realize, often at great personal cost.

There were only three things that he ever really wanted in life: to be a top golfer, to have a happy family, and to give his family comfort and security. Now, at 35, he has achieved them all.

Suddenly there is a joyous yell from the hallway — "I've got it, I've got it" — and David calls his elder son, six-year-old Andrew, to join him. Then, in the background, I hear, "Be careful, Andrew, be careful," followed by the proud statement: "This, young man, is the trophy for the US golf tournament. Your Daddy won it."

A few moments later David appears, beaming broadly and holding his trophy aloft before his family. "How about that!" he says, grinning from ear to ear. "Isn't it beautiful!"

Even if Andrew and three-year-old Michael don't quite comprehend David's uncharacteristically open display of delight, Maureen certainly does.

She's been with him through all the ups and downs of his golfing career, ever since they met at a dinner-dance in Cairns when she didn't even know golf existed. She walked every hole every day of the US Open, and is almost prouder of his achievement than he is.

Since he won the Open, David has been deluged with congratulatory letters, telegrams and phone calls. He has become an international sporting celebrity, feted at a series of special functions. On the night of our interview he and Maureen were off for an evening that crowned his success — dinner at the White House with Ronald and Nancy Reagan and Malcolm and Tamie Fraser.

Clearly the Grahams have had hardly a minute to themselves since David's spectacular three-shot win over George Burns. Although they have tried to maintain their restraint both on and off the golf course, it hasn't been easy.

"It's all been very emotional," Maureen reveals about an hour later, after her husband has finished talking and has hurried off to a lunch. "All those years of watching, and waiting and pushing. It's realizing a dream. I usually keep

The coveted US Open trophy is the pride of champion golfer David Graham.

my feelings inside — both of us do — but when he hit that birdie on the 15th I just let out the biggest scream. Then I heard myself and thought, 'Oh dear, is that really me?'

"David said he was very emotional just walking down the 18th because of the incredible applause. Then he said to himself, 'Hey, regain your composure, you've still got a two putt here.' He did it, of course, and when he saw me he suddenly realized that he'd done it. And I just hugged him very tightly.

"Then he went and signed the scorecard. I was shaking, and people were sticking microphones in my face. Words cannot express the way I felt about the win.

"The US Open is something special. I have seen this man work so hard all these years, I wanted it for him; he wanted it for us, because he has such a thing about security for families. But I wanted it so much for him."

Maureen and David have been married for 13 years, and living in America for 11, first in Florida, and now in Dallas,

8

THE AUSTRALIAN WOMEN'S WEEKLY — AUGUST 5, 1981

Australian Women's Weekly 2 page spread published 5 August 1981.

has come true!

Pictured with him are his wife, Maureen, and sons Michael, 3, and Andrew, 6.

where it took them "about three seconds" to adjust.

Although David's accent is still distinctively Australian (the local Press reports with amusement that he pronounces his name Dye-vid Grime), Maureen's speech lilts with a pronounced Southern drawl.

Maureen says her husband has mellowed in recent years, but notes that he is "still very much the male chauvinist in many ways — I haven't knocked that out of him yet."

Asked for an example she explains: "Well, he has always said women just shouldn't play golf, because it is not a lady-like sport. He says it is not lady-like for a woman to stand there with her legs apart and her behind sticking out."

David Graham knew what he wanted at 13, and he paid quite a price for it. When he left school to break into the golfing world, his father asked him to leave home as well. He has spoken to his father only once in the 21 years since.

For many years he did not drink alcohol and he had few, if any, friends, because he was always practising, practising, practising.

Then he met Maureen. "She changed me as an individual. I feel I got married so young because I was lonely, I'm not putting down my wife, but I do think that. I was very ambitious. I drove myself as hard as I possibly could. In those days I was the black sheep of the Australian golf scene because I was different from everyone else. I wasn't one of the boys, I didn't drink beer all the time and I liked to spend time alone practising my game.

"Then I met Maureen and I decided that I wanted to get married. I think I needed a friend. When I first met her, I had what everyone labelled a 'bad temper,' which I saw as an expression of frustration. I expected a lot of myself and I put a lot of pressure on myself. It seemed that everyone always passed judgement on me because of what I was like on the golf course.

"Maureen was really the first person in my life to know what I was like off the course. Apparently she came to the conclusion that I was not such a bad guy. She just worked on me — she methodically prodded and pricked at me, and made me more relaxed. She gave me confidence in myself."

David says his background wasn't nearly as bad as people may have been led to believe. "I came from what you would call a broken family — a family which in today's society would have changed the situation and said, 'Hey, it's not working out, let's part in peace'."

Although he never speaks to his father, and hasn't spoken to his sister Jennifer for 20 years, he is full of praise for his mother. "She's stuck by me through thick and thin. But in all the success I've had in golf, my mother has never seen me play golf. She absolutely refuses to go to the golf course. She's too nervous. She couldn't stand it. But I guarantee she never left the TV during the Open."

The rift with his father was caused by David's decision to be a golfer — a decision inspired by watching people practising golf as he rode his bike to school through Melbourne's Wattle Park. At 13 he had a weekend job in the Wattle Park Golf Club, and at 14 he'd organized a full-time job at the Riverdale Golf Club.

"In those days it was legal to leave school in Melbourne at 14, so I went home and told my Dad of my decision. He told me that if I left school and started work, I might as well leave home as well. And that's what happened." A year later, both he and his mother moved out.

Although David is firmly settled with his family in America, he feels strongly about golf in Australia. He has harsh words for the governing bodies, the Australian Golf Union and the Professional Golfers' Association, which, he says, are constantly at each other's throats.

This constant bickering, he claims, has alienated tournament sponsors and made it difficult for young players to get into the game.

"We have to stop this," he says, "because the future of golf is at stake."

Both the past and the future of golf mean a lot to David Graham. When I ask him what he feels is the best thing about winning the US Open, he gestures toward the trophy and replies, without a moment's hesitation.

"This is the best thing right here. When you look at this, and you see Ben Hogan, Julius Boros, Arnold Palmer, Jack Nicklaus and Lee Trevino, and especially a guy like Gary Player, you then think David Graham is among them. That's the best thing."

— SUSAN ANTHONY

Graham's determined attitude on this issue was to put him in direct, and sometimes hostile, conflict with the PGA of Australia, and, as was noted in Chapter 5, especially such senior members as Peter Thomson and Graham Marsh.

* * *

The indifferent form David Graham brought to Australia in late 1981 continued to some extent in 1982. There were a few high finishes but it took that return trip to Paris for him to record his first and only tournament victory. He defended his Lancôme Trophy title from the previous year, winning in style with another closing round in the sixties.

1983, on the other hand, was probably David Graham's most consistent year as a professional golfer. There was only one victory, in his new home state's Houston Open (Texas). A string of top five and top ten finishes saw his earnings in prize money for the calendar year stand at US$152,430. By current day standards this figure seems rather miniscule, but back then it was the most any one golfer had won in a single year. In Houston he fired his lowest ever winning round of 64, to win easily by 5 strokes from Lee Trevino, Lee Elder and Jim Thorpe.

1983 was noteworthy for another, but much sadder reason. In May of that year, 'The Boss', George Naismith died, aged 74, after a short illness. David Graham never forgot the mentoring role that Naismith had provided in his early development as a professional golfer. Also, the equally important part George played as a father figure for a young boy during his troublesome teenage years.

> **Gary fooled Naismith**
>
> Retired professional George Naismith has been showered with accolades over the years for discovering and then nurturing David Graham, the US Open champion, through his formative years in the pro shop at Riversdale. But Naismith last week admitted he wasn't the amazing judge of young golfers that some people think.
>
> At the Australian Golf Writers' Association dinner last Saturday night, Naismith, the guest speaker, disclosed that when Gary Player first came to Australia in 1956 he took one look at Player's flat rather awkward swing and said without hesitation: "That boy won't last five minutes in the game".
>
> Player, who was listening intently to Naismith's speech, said: "I guess we all make the odd mistake in our lives".
>
> **TREVOR GRANT**

Trevor Grant's report in Melbourne newspaper The Age *of the Australian Golf Writers Association dinner during the 1981 Australian Open at Victoria GC.*

Chapter 10

Nor did David's mother want the contribution of George Naismith to her son's achievements to go unheralded. She wrote a letter to *Australian Golf* magazine. This letter, which says so much about the bond between David Graham and George Naismith, is reproduced below.

"Dear Sir,

Please may I, through *Australian Golf*, pay a simple but very sincere tribute to the late Mr George Naismith.

Many will not have heard his name because that is the kind of person he was. There were so many times he could have claimed limelight but remained quietly in the wings.

He was the only man who listened to a 13-year old boy's ambition whilst others laughed. He encouraged whilst others scorned. He placed faith whilst others rubbished. Their wonderful relationship lasted exactly 24 years to the day.

During those years we all shared laughter and tears, disappointment and joy, wins and losses, as the ambition and dream became reality.

Just before his illness we planted three trees in my garden. One represents the Sportsman of the Year, another the US PGA and the third the US Open. Whilst he was planting one he said in his quiet way: "Pat, love, did you ever in your wildest dreams think we'd see it come to this? I knew he'd be good, but all this? It's incredible." Then he added: "Leave room for one for the Masters." If we are to have more future champions we must find more George Naismiths but where, goodness knows, for they are so rare.

There will be more tournaments and hopefully more wins. Perhaps the one he hoped for will come to pass but something will be missing now. The familiar voice on the phone chasing the scores and the comments always made after a televised win: "Wasn't it lovely! Did you ever see anything so sweet? He never was a basher. That's what's wrong today – bash, bash, bash."

There were times when the scores were adverse and George would take on the tone of any irate father towards a naughty boy. 'What's wrong with you boy? Settle down.'

There was never champagne after a win. Just hot scones, jam and cream and a cup of tea. But the joys we have shared, the bonds that grew, and the memories gathered are priceless and will remain long after material gains and flowery speeches have faded into oblivion.

George Naismith was unique. The trees we planted will always be there. The Boss will never be far away.

Thank you George.

Patricia Waisito (David Graham's mother), McKinnon, Victoria."

* * *

A few months after George Naismith's death, David Graham arranged for a tree to be planted, along with a memorial plaque, in front of the Riversdale Golf Club pro-shop. The tree, like those planted by his mother and Naismith, was a weeping cherry. Unfortunately the grassy slope between the pro-shop and the eighteenth green was too damp for the tree to survive. A replacement weeping cherry and the original memorial plaque can now be seen as you walk from the practice green down to the first tee.

Although a spot was left in the McKinnon garden for a 'Masters' tree the soil was destined to remain undisturbed. There was space left as well for a possible British Open triumph but that too did not eventuate.

* * *

The 1985 British Open at Royal St George's GC on the Kent coast was Graham's best chance of winning The Open. In retirement he looks back on that Championship as "the major that got away."

Always a good player in the strong winds that usually prevail on the links courses used to hold the British Opens, he had two excellent opening rounds of 68 and 71. Only Sandy Lyle could match Graham in the bleak, windy and wet conditions. Lyle's identical scores of 68 and 71 had both of them in the halfway lead.

David Graham and Sandy Lyle were the last pair out on the Saturday. Thunder, lightning and torrential rain suspended play for one hour but as the weather improved so did Graham's ball-striking. He returned a third round 70. Lyle's putting had started to fail him and his 73 left him three strokes behind the Australian. Bernhard Langer was the big

Chapter 10

AUSTRALIA'S BIG DAY IN SPORT

Great going, Graham

From BOB MacDONALD

NEW YORK, Sun. — David Graham today became the first Australian to win the U.S. Open Golf Championship.

And he did it in style with a near-perfect final round 67.

His awesome consistency had tournament veterans — including four times Open winner Jack Nicklaus — shaking their heads in amazement.

Melbourne-born Graham, 35, handled the notoriously difficult Merion course, near Philadelphia with ease.

But only by "sticking religiously" to his strategy of playing conservative golf.

"I maintained my composure all day. I never got excited. I never let my swing get out of control," Graham said.

His winning score of 273, seven under par, was one more than the Open record set by Nicklaus last year.

Graham wore down tournament leader and playing partner George Burns to take the lead on the 14th hole, then birdied the 15th to clinch victory by three strokes.

Even Burns applauded as Graham hardly faltered once on his way to the $55,000 first prize.

In Canberra, the Prime Minister, Mr Fraser, today sent congratulatory telegrams to Graham and to the Australian cricket team for winning the first Test against England.

- Full report — Back Page

THE HERALD
MELBOURNE, MONDAY, JUNE 22, 1981
FINAL EXTRA
20c
28 PAGES
358,665 daily sales

Front page headlines of The Herald in Melbourne following the 1981 US Open victory at Merion GC, Pennsylvania.

improver, his 68 tying him with Graham in the lead after 54 holes. One English commentator wrote, "No one is looking much further for a winner than Langer, this year's Masters Champion. If, however, he falters, then surely David Graham would be the man. Certainly either of these two, with a three-stroke lead, will need some catching."

The final round became a case of whoever made the least amount of errors would almost certainly win. After three early bogies, David Graham's birdies at seven and eleven took him to the outright lead with six holes to play. Playing two holes ahead of Graham and Langer, Sandy Lyle rallied, birdying the fourteenth and fifteenth holes. He was now level with Graham but when he bogeyed the difficult eighteenth it meant that David had to par the last four holes to claim victory.

"I had that Championship won with just four holes to play," he would say later. "But bogies on fifteen, sixteen and again on the last hole left me two shots shy. It was my biggest disappointment in golf as a player." "To Sandy Lyle's credit he won the tournament. I could have won but I'm grateful for the career I've had. I came out of it on the right side, twice winning majors so I have no right to say I should have won."

* * *

Despite winning golf tournaments all over the world, few victories gave David Graham as much satisfaction as winning in Australia. The prize money may have paled into insignificance when compared with most of the overseas tournaments, but for Graham the money was not the issue. What he really sought was the chance to answer the many critics he has always had in his home country. Amongst the most persistent of these have been a number of members of the Australian PGA. It was one of the reasons why his win in the 1977 Australian Open meant so much to him.

Apart from the Australian Open it was a win in the Australian Masters tournament that David Graham wanted the most. Played every year (up to 2008) at Huntingdale Golf Club in Victoria's famed sand-belt, he came close on two occasions. He was runner-up to Bernhard Langer in 1984, but it was two years later that he had his best chance to put on the winner's gold jacket.

After the first three rounds of the 1986 Australian Masters, David

Chapter 10

George Naismith (centre) enjoys a proud moment with his former assistants, David Graham and Peter Thomson. Photo, courtesy The Herald, taken at the Australian Golf Writers Association dinner during the 1981 Australian Open at Victoria GC.

Graham was well-placed, only a few strokes back from the 54 hole leader, Ian Stanley. On the back nine holes of the final round Graham made a run at Stanley, holing several birdie putts to almost draw level with him at the top of the leader-board. When Stanley bogied the long par five fourteenth he had victory in his sights. He would have won, but for two remarkable eagles by the visiting American golfer, Mark O'Meara, on the tenth and fourteenth holes. The final result was O'Meara first (284) one stroke ahead of Graham with Ian Stanley another stroke behind in third place.

Mention of Ian Stanley brings to mind their duel at Royal Melbourne in 1978. They played together in the fourth round of that year's Chrysler Classic tournament. Both were in contention to win as they teed off in the final round and their standard of play was, from the outset, of the highest quality. They matched each other shot for shot around Royal Melbourne's famous composite course.

The difference was their respective demeanours on the golf course. Graham was his usual stern and unsmiling self, concentrating fiercely on every shot and saying very little, if anything, to anyone other than his caddy. Ian Stanley was his usual self as well.

91

Known as 'the clown price of Australian golf' Stanley was out for a good time and, as he puts it, "really worked the gallery." His vaudeville show that day included a sprint, or two, down the fairway after he had hit the ball and, on another occasion, falling flat on his face after a long putt narrowly missed the cup.

In his book, *Tales of the Wandering Golfer*, Stanley wrote, "throughout this show David was not a happy man." He went on to say that when Graham "hit a sensational drive, I asked him when he was returning to America. To which he replied, 'I'd go right now if it meant that I could get away from you!'"

In the end David Graham got the bigger cheque (he finished second to the winner Billy Dunk) but Ian Stanley got the biggest ovation even though he ran third. To this day Graham is unforgiving. He maintains that Stanley's clowning around on the golf course was an unnecessary distraction for his playing partners and totally unprofessional.

* * *

There were no more tournament wins for David Graham during the latter half of the 1980's. His last 72-hole tournament win came in 1985. His win in the Queensland Open that year provided nice bookends to his professional wins as his first ever 72-hole tournament win also came in the 'Sunshine State', the 1967 Queensland PGA.

In 1990, at the relatively young age of 44, he announced his retirement from regular tournament play on the US PGA Tour.

11.

"THE SENIORS TOUR WAS MY SAVING GRACE"

After retiring from competitive golf in 1990, David Graham cut back his playing schedule considerably. His tournament play was limited to a few appearances, mainly to oblige some of his long-term sponsors and the like. In fact from 1992 through to 1996 he did not play competitively at all. He realised that his golf game had lost a lot of its sharp competitive edge. He thought it wrong for someone in his situation to take a spot away from a player who could actually win the tournament or someone who was struggling to keep his tour card or someone else trying to win enough money to get on the tour.

Those four years were the only time in Graham's life when he could play social golf and actually enjoy it. He played during his late forties on Saturday mornings at his club in Dallas, the exclusive, men only, Preston Trail Golf Club.

Many professionals find it difficult to play social golf because they are used to playing at a very high intensity level. To go from the pressures and stresses of tournament golf, to playing relaxed social four-balls is a transition they are not comfortable with. Another factor is the high expectation placed on professionals by the general golfing public. This expectation invariably extends well into a professional golfer's retirement years.

David Graham was fortunate that his regular foursome did not expect major winning form each time he teed it up at Preston Trail. He appreciated that they were not judgmental about the drive he hit into the trees or the shot that didn't carry the water hazard or whatever. They didn't care if he shot 71 or 81 and, with their handicaps, David used to lose US$10 every Saturday morning anyway.

All this changed as he approached his fiftieth birthday. The US Seniors Tour (now known as the Champions Tour) beckoned. "I had to refocus," he said. "I was supposed to be a pretty good player. If you have pride in your performances and are going to play competitive golf you have to be focused." The regular practice routines returned and he adopted a physical fitness regime aimed at having him ready, not just to compete, but win on the Seniors Tour.

Being eligible for the Seniors Tour in 1996 was crucial to David Graham's self-esteem which suffered a massive hit towards the middle of that year. As a result of a player-led revolt, Graham was replaced as non-playing captain of the 1996 Presidents Cup Team. The Champions Tour was his way back during that difficult period. He channeled his disappointment, indeed his anger, into preparing for and playing in that year's Seniors Tour events. Speaking in 1999 he put it this way "I think the Seniors Tour has been my saving grace, as have a lot of the players on the Seniors Tour been my saving grace."

* * *

In his first three years on the Champions Tour, David Graham won four times, racking up total prize money of just over US$4 million in the process. The most memorable of those four victories was in the 1998 Royal Caribbean Classic played at Crandon Park Golf Club in Key Biscayne, Florida. There, in the last round, and especially over the closing holes, he showed he had not lost his ability to 'go low' when the tournament was on the line. Several strokes back with only three holes to play, he birdied all three of them to force a play-off with Dave Stockton.

Their sudden death play-off created history. After nine holes of the play-off, in which Graham and Stockton matched each other with pars and birdies, David Graham hit his approach on the tenth play-off hole to within a foot (30cm) of the cup. His tap-in birdie putt won the hole and broke the US PGA Tour and Seniors Tour record for the longest extra hole play-off. The record had been set the previous year at Newport Beach Golf Club in California when Bob Murphy prevailed over Jay Sigel on the ninth extra hole to claim the Toshiba Classic. David Graham won a fifth title in 2001 and played regularly on the Champions Tour until 2004.

* * *

Chapter 11

Near the end of his playing career on the Seniors Tour.

During the latter stages of his playing days on the PGA Tour and in the first five or six years of his retirement David Graham moved into golf course design. Like a lot of professional golfers he saw this as "a fitting extension" to his golf career.

Graham formed a partnership with a fellow designer, Gary Panks. He would be the first to admit that Panks was the principal designer, the one who laid out the routing plans and was responsible for the engineering specifications. So what was David Graham's role? "I was a critic and a follower", he would say in describing his architectural function. With his trademark honesty he summed up the contribution of professional golfers to the course design process as "essentially we are there to advise and suggest. The real work is done by others, experts in their particular fields. What the professional does provide is his name. It is assumed that his well known name will endow a new golf course with a certain prestige and status."

In the 10 or so years that David Graham was involved in his course design partnership he put his name to more than twenty golf courses worldwide. The majority of them in America.

In Australia he is best known for his layout in coastal Queensland at Laguna Quays adjacent to the Whitsunday Islands and the Great Barrier Reef. Opened in 1992, the course (named Turtle Point) was regarded by many as the best layout in Queensland and it was regularly ranked well inside the top fifty golf courses in the entire country. For various commercial and political reasons the course and residential development are now defunct.

Talking in 1990, Graham revealed that he would like to build a tournament golf course in Australia where spectators could view golf in comfort, something along the lines of an American Tournament Players Championship (TPC) course. Recognising that the older traditional courses in Australia were wonderful to play, he noted that they are not very good for large galleries. "They are too confined, so hopefully I will be able to build a tournament-type course that may be good enough to one day hold an Australian Open. That I would really like." Retiring from course design in 1996, to concentrate on his foray into the Seniors circuit, this dream did not eventuate. A tournament style course that catered for gallery viewing was built in Australia in 2001 and it did go on to host the 2003 and 2005 Australian Opens. It was the Open Course at Moonah Links on Victoria's Mornington Peninsula. The designer was Graham's old 'adversary', Peter Thomson.

David Graham described his golf course design philosophy as, "I don't really have one." Perhaps he was saying that each design was dependant on the available land, and flexibility was therefore essential. Ultimately the new course is "dictated by the guy with the cheque book. You have to look at it as a business. If the gentleman who is spending millions of dollars says, 'Build me (say) the hardest golf course in the world', you say, "Yes, Sir."

Nevertheless Graham does have two "cornerstones" when it comes to new courses. He has a major fetish with bunkers and the way they are built. He insists that they be flat-bottomed and not too difficult to play out. The other concern he has is with so-called 'signature holes'. "When someone says 'Wait till you get to the 15th hole, it's our signature hole', what does that make the other 17, chopped liver?"

* * *

In 1993, David Graham was appointed to the six-man Cup and Tee Committee at the US Masters. It is an honourary position that means a great deal to him and one that he puts "a tremendous amount of time and effort into." Not surprisingly, Graham has vigourously defended the Committee's role in selecting the hole positions on Augusta's severely sloping greens. He says the claims that the greens are 'tricked up' during Masters Week are "so far from the truth, it's unbelievable." He maintains that "there are very subtle little shelves on most of those greens, and it takes a while to get to know them. In some cases if you move the hole 12 inches (30cm) to the left, or right, it would become unfair because the hole would then be on the edge of the shelf." To emphasise this point he noted that "the pin positions the Augusta members play are far more difficult than what the tournament pins are."

Reflecting, in 2011, on his nearly twenty years on the Cup and Tee Committee at Augusta he repeated how honoured he was to be asked each year to serve on the Committee. Their prime aim each year is to make sure that the hole locations are fair, relevant to the speed of the greens and of course the expected weather conditions, especially the strength and direction of forecasted winds. He stressed that equipment changes of recent years, such as ball quality, long distance drivers and grooves on irons do not, contrary to the opinion of some, come into the equation when setting daily hole locations. "The weather has far more of a bearing, but then there are some traditional fourth day pins, like at holes 12 and 16, which we don't deviate from." The Committee, under David Graham's supervision, does not set the pin positions in advance for all four days of the tournament. Unlike many other PGA tournaments, the decisions relating to individual hole placements are made on a daily basis.

12.

"I CRIED. I CRIED ABSOLUTELY. SO DID MY WIFE".

The inaugural Presidents Cup was held in mid-September 1994 at the Robert Trent Jones Golf Club in Gainesville, Virginia. Closely resembling the Ryder Cup format, it pitted an American team of professional golfers against a team of International golfers. The Internationals could come from any country other than Great Britain and Europe from which representatives were selected to compete every two years against the Americans for the Ryder Cup. It appears that there was some opposition to the staging of another team match play contest from some regular members of the US Ryder Cup team. They were reluctant to commit to such a competition in those years in which the Ryder Cup was not played.

The Presidents Cup took a lot of work to establish and David Graham, as the first non-playing Captain of the International team, put in many hours himself. He was heavily involved, along with the Captain of the US team, Hale Irwin, in the pre-tournament promotion of the event.

The budget for the 1994 Presidents Cup was quite meagre and David Graham feels that he most likely got the job as Captain of the Internationals because he was a resident of the US. This would save the organisers considerable time and money by not having to fly a non-resident back and forth to America for the many planning meetings that were necessary to set up the staging of the event.

There was much for him and Hale Irwin to do. For instance, decisions had to be made about which players would be eligible for selection on the International team, on what criteria they would be chosen and how many Captain's picks would be allowed. As Graham recalls, "We didn't even have a logo and no-one even knew what the team colours would be."

The first contest resulted in a comfortable win for the US team, but the whole event was an undoubted success and everyone involved looked forward to the second Presidents Cup scheduled at the same venue for September 1996. David Graham was again asked to serve as captain and agreed to do so.

* * *

David Graham had no real intention to back up as Internationals Captain in 1996. He only accepted the invitation when he learned that the Americans were to be led by Arnold Palmer, with whom Graham had a long and mutually respectful friendship. The catch-cry for the second staging of the Presidents Cup was to be, 'a President (George Bush Senior), a King (Arnold Palmer) and a Captain (David Graham)'.

What exactly happened in the months leading up to the 1996 Cup is still something of a mystery. It is known that a player revolt led to David Graham's removal as captain of the International team just before the event was due to begin. Graham was replaced, as Captain, by his golfing nemesis, Peter Thomson.

To get a better understanding of the dramatic events surrounding the 1996 Presidents Cup, it is useful to take note of the comments made at that time by some of the chief protagonists as well as those of several 'interested observers'.

David Graham was obviously very concerned about the circumstances that led to him being forced to resign from the captaincy and with good reason, he was also concerned about the role Greg Norman played in the situation.

A few weeks before the Cup was due to start, Norman stated, "We're all very concerned (about Graham's organisational abilities). It's like walking into a room full of fog. You don't know what the heck's going on. You've got to get the team camaraderie going early. It's like we're not even playing a golf tournament."

In 1994 Norman had been forced to withdraw from the Cup when he had haemorrhoid surgery. When he came to the course on the last day the event telecasters, CBS, asked him to wear a microphone as he went round supporting the Internationals. They thought his comments would add valuable insight to their telecast commentary, and the proposal was put to David Graham.

"The Presidents Cup is not Greg Norman's tournament. It's a twelve man team, it's not Greg's team", he said as he refused the CBS request.

At some stage either prior to the Presidents Cup or in the weeks following the 1996 event, Graham received a phone call from Norman. According to Graham, and admitted to later by Norman, the call was an attempt to convince Graham that he had not instigated Graham's departure.

It is important to note that David Graham did receive considerable support over how he was treated. One supporter was Gary Player. In describing the way the International players handled the situation Player said, "it was a total disgrace, a humiliating embarrassment for Graham which had also damaged the image of the game."

Frank Williams, Greg Norman's manager at the time, was surprised when Norman was made the scapegoat for Graham's resignation. According to Williams, "At a meeting of the International team members held during July's British Open (in 1996) apparently one player started complaining, 'Well, David never tells us anything and he's so arrogant and he made my wife leave in the middle of a banquet" (at the White House in 1994) and then another guy chipped in and then they all chipped in and they all had their own little grievances about Graham."

"A lot of guys were gunning for him," wrote Michael Clayton. "He'd pissed off Ernie Els because he had criticised Ernie the time before for not playing (in the 1994 Cup) when Ernie had committed to play in that year's Dunhill Cup, and it's pretty hard to piss off Ernie. As well, a lot of guys, when they came back from the first Presidents Cup, said he hadn't done that great a job."

Speaking from Lexington, Kentucky, on the eve of the 1996 Presidents Cup competition, where he was contesting a Seniors event, David Graham did not hold back in expressing how he felt about the so-called 'sacking'. His remarks were immediately picked up and reported in the widely read national newspaper, *USA Today*, where Graham singled out Greg Norman as the instigator of his dismissal. He demanded an apology from all of the International team members and went on to say, "I hope the US team wins the Cup for what the members of the International team have done to me."

Needless to say, this last comment did not go down well with the

International team. Following the presentation ceremony at the end of the 1996 Cup, New Zealander, Frank Nobilo, let known his sentiments about Graham. He labeled Graham's Cup eve remarks as "treason-like". "Personally, I was extremely disappointed with what I read in the *USA Today* newspaper several days ago. With what happened a couple of months ago, and a lot of negative press between now and then, the guys (on the team) felt they had no support because everyone else was going against them. What he said is something I would never stoop to. We did try to use Graham's remarks to fire ourselves up and, given a slightly different set of circumstances, it might have made the difference, but we had a great team and we had a great team captain."

Not surprisingly Greg Norman backed up Nobilo. "The team factor was phenomenal. It just goes to show you the heart and courage of some people. Our team camaraderie was just so great, our captain (Peter Thomson) plus our co-captain, Ian Baker-Finch, did a great job."

The 'complaining' player referred to by Frank Williams was the Australian, Steve Elkington. Elkington was still angry with Graham over a 1994 Presidents Cup incident. That year Elkington's pregnant wife had wanted to leave early from a pre-tournament reception for both teams at The White House, in Washington. It appears that she wanted the entire International Team to leave with her and her husband in the middle of the State reception, "So as," she said, "my husband and I wouldn't appear rude." David Graham quickly told her "You've got to be kidding me". According to him he then offered to get her "a car or a limousine" to take them home. But Graham noted at the time, "Steve was really riled by this".

Never one to deny his share of any blame for 'incidents' that have occurred during his career, David Graham admits that on the morning after the White House dinner he definitely did slip up. He made a comment to someone on the team bus along the lines of, "some b-i-t-c-h, who was a guest of the White House, wanted to tell the President that the dinner was (prematurely) over". It turned out that Mrs Elkington was in the seat just behind Graham's and was, naturally, very upset by the remark.

As well, it would seem that another 1994 team member still bore Graham a grudge from that year. Ernie Els, who missed the 1994 Cup, despite being selected in the team, because of another tournament commitment, was upset by David Graham's remark, "I hope those who skipped the Presidents Cup would regret it for the rest of their lives".

Bruce Devlin, Graham's long-time friend, was another who vigorously defended David. "Greg Norman was the source (of the player mutiny)", he stated. "Finchem," he continued, "could have stood by him but he folded like a tent. No guts! I just thought the whole thing was totally classless".

Tim Finchem was the Commissioner of the USPGA Tour, the body responsible for the organisation of the 1994 and 1996 Presidents Cups. He was, and still is, one of the most influential figures in tournament golf, world-wide.

"Devlin doesn't know what he's talking about," Norman responded. "He wasn't even in the room for the players' meeting about their captain. For him to say that I was the source is categorically untrue."

* * *

The "players' meeting" referred to by Greg Norman was convened at Royal Lytham-St Annes just prior to the (July) 1996 British Open by Mike Bodney of the US PGA. The purpose of the meeting, according to an International team member of the first Presidents Cup, was to discuss (among other matters) the arrangements for the 1996 Presidents Cup to be held about eight weeks later. He stated that the meeting was "perfectly routine" and intended to provide general information to those eligible International players at the Open before final selection of the team was made.

When the matter of International Team Captain was raised, Greg Norman and Frank Nobilo pointedly enquired as to where David Graham was. This initiated much debate, both for and against Graham retaining the captaincy. There was an expression of no-confidence and it was decided to take a vote. Of the (about) twenty International players present, one abstained while the majority voted to replace him.

This created an urgent problem for Bodney who, disturbed by this sudden development, immediately contacted Peter Thomson to fill the vacancy. Thomson declined at first, but agreed later although he "felt bad about it". At their first team meeting, he "lectured them on the unfairness of what they had done" and today, when asked about the Graham dismissal, says it was a "very cruel thing that happened to him."

On 1 August 1996, an article by leading Australian golf writer, Peter Stone, appeared in the *Sydney Morning Herald* headed "I'm guilty of nothing, retorts puzzled Graham". See Appendix III.

Like Devlin, Lee Trevino pointed the finger directly at Tim Finchem. "I blame Finchem," he said. "Finchem wouldn't go to bat for David Graham, which is why I couldn't support them when several years later (in 2008) the USPGA Tour asked me to be a Presidents Cup captain. I said to them, hell no! I'm still pissed off about it."

David Graham recognised that Norman and Elkington were "very prominent players at that time" but regrets that the Australian PGA didn't show any support for him, "so the players got what they wanted and I stepped down." Soon after, Graham withdrew his membership of the Australian PGA and said, "it was hard for me to be a member of something that does not make you feel welcome."

Trevino had experience as a losing team captain himself. In 1985 he captained the American Team that was trounced by the Europeans in the Ryder Cup. Like Graham, Trevino pulled no punches when talking to, or about, his players. His criticism of them after their 1985 defeat remains one of the biggest sprays ever given in international teams golf. "To tell you the truth", he said, "I thought they were a bunch of cry-babies and I told them that. I can't play for them, but the way some of them were playing I could have probably given them four (holes) a side and still they would have got the socks beat off them."

Since 1996 David Graham has talked to only a few of that year's International team. When asked if the players he talked to were the ones he suspected as having a hand in his dismissal he replied, "No, they were not. With the exception of a couple of phone calls from Greg Norman." He went on to say that several players had called him "to express their displeasure about what had happened. A couple of them told me they weren't even at the meeting (in which the players agreed to seek Graham's dismissal). From what I understand it wasn't a unanimous vote."

Asked if he thought the truth as to exactly what happened would eventually come out, David Graham was philosophical. "There have been so many conflicting stories that I don't even know what could be right or what is actually right. I don't think anybody will openly admit they were the culprit. I do think there were more people involved than one person, but that's strictly speculation."

When asked if he felt that one day he could forgive 'the collaborators', Graham was very measured in his response. "I won't ever forgive them. I've often said that the wound is healed, but the scar is still there. I was particularly disappointed in the few of them I had known for twenty odd years. To all of them I would most likely just like to say, "Stay out of my life. Stay away!"

The deep hurt felt by David Graham is evident in these poignant memories. "When I heard that I had been ousted from the 1996 Cup, I cried. To get toward the end of your career and have certain people start slamming your reputation and your credibility, you take it personally. I cried, absolutely. So did my wife."

He went on, "If you looked at the history of the Ryder Cup, I'm sure there were some great captains and some not-so-good captains. But it's hard to imagine Gary Player or Bruce Devlin, two of the game's great ambassadors, taking the action that was taken against me. I think they would have sat down and said, 'Look guys, I think we need to think this through a little bit more. This is someone's reputation and this is an extremely important golf tournament. We can't attack somebody like that. It accomplishes nothing.'"

"You can't chop and change captains at will on the word of somebody who happens to be a good player at that time. Players come and go, and just because they have their four or five years in the spotlight doesn't mean they should be allowed to dictate policy."

David Graham is a hard-edged character, "irredeemably stubborn, blunt and dogmatic," as one writer once described him. This hard edge that saw him refuse to acquiesce to his players' demands in 1994 and 1996 undoubtedly contributed, rightly or wrongly, to his demise as captain for the second Presidents Cup. That "flinty interior", as another writer described it, certainly helped establish Graham as one of the top players in the world during the late 1970s and into the early 1980s. But it didn't serve him well in the very different role of non-playing captain of a team of very diverse, often ego-driven, individuals.

Irrespective of the blame, if any, that can be attributed to some team members and/or administrators, one thing is clear. The whole episode could have been handled much better. "It could have been handled in such an easier, less embarrassing way," Graham reflected years later, "not only for myself but also for the Presidents Cup."

* * *

Talking to David Graham in 2008, Cameron Morfit, a golf writer of many years experience said, "It's hard to square Graham's reputation as an overly exacting curmudgeon, which became etched in stone after his downfall as Presidents Cup captain, with the man today. He calls the 1996 episode "disgraceful" and even questioned the Tour's decision to appoint Greg Norman as the 2009 captain, but his heart isn't in it anymore."

As recent evidence of this viewpoint of Morfit's, David Graham has himself said, "I would like to think there were many other things of importance, such as my life or my career, rather than the Presidents Cup. Everybody knows it was a bad deal but I think it's just best for me to say it's over with, it's history."

For the record the US team won the 1996 Presidents Cup. After the Friday four-balls and foursomes with the Americans leading 7½ to 2½ matches, everyone, said Norman, "had written us off". The Internationals fought back on day two, narrowing the US lead to just one match (10½ to 9½). A tense final day saw both teams share the twelve singles matches (6 each) to enable the US to successfully defend the Cup. Late on the final day, Fred Couples, birdied the seventeenth hole in his match, to shut out Vijay Singh, and secure the American team's vital cup winning point. It remains the closest the Internationals have come to beating the Americans on their home turf.

There is an interesting, if not ironic, postscript to David Graham's Presidents Cup story. In March 2011 Graham was appointed to the executive committee of the Presidents Cup. Unsure as to what his duties would be if he travelled to Australia for the November 2011 contesting of the Cup at Royal Melbourne Golf Club, "other than to stand around, but that's fine," he hoped his health issues would allow him to be there.

Even after his appointment to the executive committee, David

Graham reiterated, in May 2011, his preference for "an apology for the loss of the 1996 captaincy from Greg Norman, plus one from Steve Elkington, who did all the dirty work for Norman."

On the way to Melbourne, David Graham spent some time in Sydney where he caught up with several representatives of former Federal Sports Minister, John Brown's, charitable foundation. This foundation raises money for the purchase of wheel chairs for children who need them but can't afford them. Every year Graham donates some tickets for the US Masters to the foundation. These tickets are sold to the highest bidder, so to speak, and when the recipients are in Augusta, David Graham is their host for what is truly a memorable week.

David Graham was able to attend the 2011 Presidents Cup, where he took up his position as an 'Official Observer' of the four-day contest, a role he shared with the man who replaced him as International Team Captain in 1996, Peter Thomson. In fact, one of Graham's motivations to attend the Presidents Cup that year was to convey a personal message to Thomson.

* * *

During his visit to Melbourne for the Presidents Cup, David Graham returned to Riversdale Golf Club, where he was awarded life membership. At a brief ceremony beside the tree, planted to honour George Naismith's thirty-four years as club professional, Graham paid tribute to his mentor for his guidance and friendship. Of interest was David's reference to George as 'Mr Naismith', such is his great respect for his 'old boss'.

On a tour of Riversdale's course, David Graham was asked by Club Captain, Jonathan McCleary, to "have a go" at hitting a ball onto the third green, a par three hole of 148 metres (163 yards). A right-handed club was on hand and David had no trouble in doing just that. He was then asked to try and repeat the task, this time with a left-handed seven iron. Again Graham was able to find the heart of the green with his tee shot.

It was appropriate for David to use the third hole to display his two-sided ability, for just a few metres (yards) away, is the practice tee, where exactly fifty years earlier, a young David Graham first made the switch from left-handed to right-handed.

13.

"IT WAS THE END OF ME AS A GOLFER — IT WAS ALMOST THE END OF ME, FULL STOP!"

In June 2004, David Graham teed off in the Seniors tour Bank of America Championship in Boston. He never made it past the eighth hole of Sunday's final round.

David had developed a cough earlier that week but decided to "just play through it." He got through Friday's opening round and despite feeling no better, completed 18 holes on Saturday. On Sunday he felt even worse. On the eighth green his caddie told him that he looked awful and that he should go in. Graham's reply was along the lines of "Hang on I'll just hit this putt." But he never did. Standing over the ball he collapsed.

David Graham was rushed to hospital. Starting the day in golf spikes he ended it in a hospital gown. He spent five days there. He heart was diseased and pumping at only 12% of its normal volume. The official diagnosis was congestive heart failure, cardiomyopathy, "and one or two other things." The big muscles and small muscles of his heart weren't working together as they should. There was nothing much the doctors could do except to manage the condition with medication. Talking about it two years later he said, "it was the end of me as a golfer. It was almost the end of me, full stop!"

From that point on David Graham's life took a dramatic "sharp turn left." His daily diet now included a regimen of fruits and vegetables along with a "fistful of pills." Graham had been a smoker since his teenage years but had kicked the habit some three years earlier. It had not been easy. "In terms of difficulty, quitting was about as easy as winning the US Open", was his assessment of the task.

Like many people faced with a life-changing illness or injury, David Graham experienced several months of depression. This 'why me?' state lasted the best part of six months. The turning point was a television program about a children's hospital. A five-year old cancer patient was being interviewed. The little girl, smiling at the interviewer said, "I can choose to be sick and unhappy or I can choose to be sick and happy. I choose to be happy." That was her personal choice and it became David Graham's as well.

* * *

After his collapse in Boston, a year went by without Graham even so much as holding a golf club. Now residing at Whitefish, Montana, it was a member friend at Iron Horse Golf Club in Whitefish who enticed him back to the golf course. The friend needed a partner for a four-ball event and he persuaded David to team up with him for the two-day event. He was able to use a cart but the first nine holes on the Saturday were memorable for all the wrong reasons.

David Graham's opening tee shot went all of eighty yards (73m). He hit the turf a good four inches (10cm) behind the ball. On the fourth hole, a par 5, he was forty yards (36m) short of the green in two but finished with an eleven! On the par three seventh he shanked his tee shot so far right it disappeared into the adjoining woods. He claimed that this was the first shank he had ever hit. "Man, was it embarrassing. Now I understand what all the fuss is about them."

The next day was better but the upshot of the whole experience was, for Graham, the end of the line. He gave away most of his clubs "except the irons I used to win the PGA and the Open and the bull's-eye putter I used at Merion." He also "threw fifteen pairs of golf shoes into the dump", vowing never to play again.

For somebody who always "just loved to play" it was a bitter pill to swallow. No longer would he "get up at two o'clock in the morning and excitedly go out to the workshop", grab a shaft, a club head and a grip and make a putter before going back to bed an hour or so later. Gone was that feeling of anticipation the next morning that perhaps "it was going to be the best putter I ever had."

In fact David Graham did play again in competition. It was late in 2010 and he was a member of a three-man scramble team that played in a fund-raiser 18-hole event immediately prior to that year's 3M

Tournament on the Champions (Seniors) Tour. But Graham is quick to squash any talk of his return to golf. "That was the first time I have done something like that in seven years," he said at the 2011 Masters Tournament. "The fact that it was an exhibition to raise money for a very worthwhile charity and that Lee Trevino and Arnold Palmer were there, persuaded me to have a hit. But a three man scramble is not my definition of playing golf, but it was a good cause, I was well taken care of, and thoroughly enjoyed myself."

* * *

Since 2010 Graham's golf has been restricted to hitting a few balls on the range and playing the occasional round with friends at Iron Horse Golf Club in Montana. When he holidays in California, usually during the very cold winters of Montana, he plays golf with Arnold Palmer. "He (Palmer) doesn't like me as an opponent", he confided in 2011, "because I outdrive him. But he putts better than I do. Heck, we're just a couple of old guys who still like to hit it around."

It is not unusual for first time major winners to retire the clubs they used to win. David Graham certainly did, but little-known American golf professional, Rives McBee, took club retirement to the extreme. McBee stunned everyone, including himself, by setting a course record 64 at the Olympic Club in San Francisco in the first round of the 1996 US Open. McBee's lead was short-lived and he finished well back in the field by the Championship's end. "I had my fifteen minutes of fame," he recalled in 1997. "When I got home from that Open, I put the golf bag and the clubs I'd used inside my house and never used them again. That's how special they were."

These days David Graham is almost unrecognisable from the man he was in the seventies and eighties. He is twenty pounds heavier than he was in his prime. His face, once 'hawk-like', is now fleshier. But his eyes still have that steely glint in them and there is still some vestige of the much broader Australian accent of thirty years ago.

While medication has stabilised his cardiomyopathy, his weak heart limits his physical activity. Graham can walk on level ground but must be careful that his heart doesn't beat more than 100 times a minute.

A recent photograph revealing the ravages of time and illness.

David Graham, the one time hard man of professional golf, now cries a lot. His wife Maureen says it is a side effect of the many pills he takes each day but, by his own admission, Graham has developed a sensitive side. "All my life", he said in 2006, "I fought like the devil to be successful, to escape the terrible start I had in life and build a much better life for my wife and children. I pushed all the time and, one day, I almost died and missed the very things I'd worked for. All of the goodness (in my life) has hit me all at once. Yes, he concurred, "I've become very sensitive, a baby really. Now every time I turn around I'm living the end of a really happy movie."

As for his reputation as a 'hard man' David Graham, not surprisingly, disagrees. "I'm honest, sure, and to the point if I don't like something, I'll certainly say so. I see things pretty much black and white." Despite the contrary opinion of some, Graham feels that he had actually learned to restrain himself over the past ten years or so. Even more revealing is his 1999 admission that he "wished I could retract some of the things I've said in the past" because they were "things I never really meant, they were construed the wrong way due to the way I said them."

* * *

Talking about his new life in Montana, David Graham observes that the friendships he has made in Whitefish are considerably different from the friendships he had on tour. They were not founded or built around golf and that made it very challenging for him. "Forming these new friendships is like learning to walk", he said a few years back. "That's because they are rooted in everyday lives that cover the gamut."

Graham felt that in this respect they contrasted to the rather narrow basis of friendships made on tour. "The friendships made on tour", he said, "are more like acquaintances because of the transient yet highly focused life we professional golfers all lead."

Graham has several friendships from his playing days that go beyond the acquaintance level. He regularly talks on the phone with Bruce Devlin and Tom Weiskopf, or 'Big T', as Graham affectionately calls him. Another long-standing friend is Lee Trevino.

For quite a few years both Graham and Trevino lived in Dallas, Texas. They became firm friends, even sharing an aeroplane for much of that time, flying to and from tournaments. David Graham attributed Lee Trevino for encouraging him to relax more, both on and off the golf course. In a 2011 interview with Jim Webster, for *Golf Australia* magazine, Graham said that as a result of much travelling with Trevino, he "learned to laugh a lot more, eat Mexican food, watch old John Wayne movies and not get too much sleep in the process!"

"He is like me", Trevino claims. "He came to America with nothing but his trade and determination. He too was an outsider who had to play his way in." Trevino probably saw something of himself in David Graham. "Being where I'm at now", he said recently, "from where I came from, not knowing my father, spending a few years in the Marine Corps, coming out to work at a golf club in Dallas, not as a professional but on the maintenance crew, to six and a half years later, winning the US Open. If that's not an achievement I don't know what is." He concluded with a statement that could well have come from David Graham himself. "That's what I'm (most) proud of, doing it on pure guts, on my own, to get where I am today." David Graham would probably temper such a claim with due recognition to the likes of Bruce Devlin, George Naismith and his wife Maureen and the help they provided him along the way.

14.

"HOW DO YOU PUT ISAO AOKI IN BEFORE DAVID GRAHAM?"

His golf career now behind him David Graham can sit back and reflect on numerous achievements. For so long, the idea of 'sitting back' was foreign to him, but times have changed. Relaxing on the porch of his home in Whitefish, Montana, or at the local gun club after some skeet shooting is, these days, very much par for the course.

As for reflection there is much that should gratify him. His 35 professional victories included wins in Australia, Asia, Africa, Europe and South America as well as North America. In the United States he won 13 times on the PGA Tour and the Champions Tour. He was a member of Dunhill and World Cup winning teams and played a significant role in getting the biennial Presidents Cup up and running.

Yet two snubs by those in golfing officialdom must surely linger as sore points. The first of these, the so-called mutiny at the 1996 Presidents Cup, is irredeemable. The other, Graham's continued exclusion from Golf's Hall of Fame, is not.

For many years David Graham said little about his non-inclusion in the Hall of Fame but Bruce Devlin has repeatedly expressed his opinion that in this respect Graham "has got a raw deal." As Devlin points out, David Graham is the only Australian to have won two of golf's four majors, the PGA Championship and the United States Open. Certainly Peter Thomson won five majors and Greg Norman two but all seven of those wins came in the same major, the British Open.

Four Australians — Jim Ferrier, Steve Elkington, Wayne Grady and, most recently, Geoff Ogilvy, have won one major in the United States but only David Graham has triumphed in two of the three majors played each year in America.

Devlin's argument for Graham's inclusion is sound. Indeed, Graham's record would seem to be comparable to many of the other inductees. It could even be argued that it is superior to some of them. Bruce Devlin, in emphasising this point, once said, somewhat caustically, "Some people in there got in with less of a record than him. How do you put Isao Aoki (the first Japanese golfer to win on the European and American PGA Tours) in the Hall of Fame before David Graham?"

In 2011, Graham was more outspoken when asked about his continued exclusion from The Hall of Fame. "It is," he said, "embarrassing and I think it shows the inadequacies that exist in it when some players are getting in without winning any major championships because they're from certain countries. I also don't think golf course designers should be in the Hall of Fame, it should be reserved for players only."

David Graham admitted, "It is a thorn in my side. I consider the voting system is at fault. Either that, or I have offended someone, like (US Tour Commissioner) Finchem." As to his decision to speak out publicly for the first time about The Hall of Fame, he claims that his airing of these grievances is for no personal gain. His statement, "At this stage of my life my bringing attention to it," serves to highlight the feelings of a lot of players. Graham cited two-time major champion, Sandy Lyle, as someone who should definitely be in the Hall of Fame. Unlike other players voted in from the International category, he points out that Lyle frequently tested himself against the best players in the world, on the US PGA Tour and elsewhere.

In 2012, Graham's 'prediction' was realised. Sandy Lyle joined Phil Mickelson and Hollis Stacy as inductees to the World Golf Hall of Fame. Once again David Graham was overlooked. As golf writer Paul Prendergast correctly pointed out, "David Graham's career record compares extremely favourably with Lyle's, even more so when you dig a little deeper to compare consistency of performances in majors."

"A comparison between Graham and Sandy Lyle," Prendergast notes, "shows that while both won two majors, Graham achieved an additional fourteen top ten placings across all four majors whilst Lyle achieved only two, both at the British Open."

Prendergast concluded with a hope, shared by all Australians, that "surely, the frustrating wait will be over soon for the man deserving of a place in the Hall of Fame alongside fellow Aussies Peter Thomson, Kel Nagle, Greg Norman and Karrie Webb?"

Graham's final word on the subject is 'pure David Graham'. "I have no interest in being in it when I'm dead. If it's going to happen (for me) they'd better do it while I'm alive, I'm not (having) my family there when I'm gone!"

* * *

As a young golfer starting out on 'the big show' (the USPGA Tour), David Graham committed himself enthusiastically to America and the American way of life. From his first home in Florida through to a more permanent base in Dallas, Texas, and more recently in the 'Big Sky' State of Montana, he came to call the United States home. "I will be forever grateful for what golf in the United States has given me," he said way back in January 1982. More significantly he went on to declare, "I have no intention of ever leaving America."

At the same time David Graham was conscious of his Australian background. When asked if he was still eager to be known as an Australian, Graham's reply was two edged. "Parts of it make me proud (when I recall them), like my years at Riversdale with George Naismith. But there are quite a few other parts of it I'd just as soon forget." On a lighter note David yearns for "a meat pie and some really good fish and chips."

Seventeen years later, in 1999, David Graham reiterated his appreciation of the United States. "Pretty much everything I have today I got in America. Pretty much all my friends today are in America and this is definitely where I'll spend the rest of my life. Both my sons are United States citizens and I will become one too one day." True to his word, David Graham is, in addition to his Australian citizenship, now a United States citizen and very much at home in America.

Although David Graham hasn't publicly stated it, one suspects that the usual bonds of family and friends that tie many Australians who live abroad to Australia don't have the same attraction for David Graham. His bitter separation from his father at such an early age and the loss of contact in subsequent years with his mother and sister, for whatever reason, undoubtedly contributed to Graham still calling America (and not Australia) home.

As well, his feisty and, at times, belligerent attitude as a young professional in Australia did not endear him to those he came in contact with both on and off Australian golf courses. It is also, perhaps, why David Graham has not received the same recognition for his golfing feats in Australia that he is afforded in the United States. In America his status as a golfer is well known and he sits comfortably alongside fellow Australians Greg Norman and Peter Thomson. In Australia I suspect the general sporting public knows something of him but not the full extent of his achievements over a forty-year career.

APPENDIX I

PRECISION GOLF FORGING PTY LTD   27-43 HILES STREET   ALEXANDRIA NSW   AUSTRALIA
CABLES HANDFORGE SYDNEY   69 5041

DG/HM   20th March, 1968.

Mr. G. Naismith,
Professional,
Melbourne Sports Depot,
55 Elizabeth Street,
MELBOURNE.......VIC. 3000.

Dear Mr. Naismith,

    Firstly, may I say thank you very much for your encouragement during the Victorian Open. The last round proved a little disappointing but I feel sure through the experience I gained in that particular round playing with Nagle and Thomson I came out on the right side of things.

    It certainly was a pleasure playing with you again and I hope that when I come back to Melbourne you may be able to arrange another game, possibly a social game rather than playing under the pressure of tournament play.

    I have a little item of news which I am sure will interest you. Last week a private businessman in N.S.W. offered me an amazing contract. I approached the heads of P.G.F. and they assured me that I would be making the right decision if I accepted it. The contract guarantees me a considerable amount of money over the next three (3) years, plus all my air fares and expenses, plus a motor car whilst in N.S.W. I have been told that the contact is one of the best, considering my age and the little I have done in tournament golf. I will also be on a contract with P.G.F. over three (3) years for using their equipment. They have also offered a golf ball contract, plus an annual retainer for the next 3 years, with a clause in the contract that if I win a major tournament it will automatically be open for renewal.

    So you can see that since the Victorian Open things have really been going my way. I hope that in the next two or three years, through the amount of practise and dedication I will be applying to my golf, I may do my sponsor the credit he deserves.

    I was very pleased to see Mrs. Naismith on the final day and for a moment I found it a little hard to recognise her as it had been a few years since I had seen her. May I say that

UNITED KINGDOM   PHILIPPINES   USA   NEW ZEALAND   HONGKONG

PRECISION GOLF FORGING
PTY LTD

Page 2

she looks in as good health as you do.

I hope that you are pleased with the news in this letter as I feel playing under the new circumstances will make me be more relaxed and I will be able to concentrate a little more on golf rather than the financial side of the game.

I will close now and look forward to seeing you in the very near future.

Lots of love and good fishing,

David Graham

Appendix I

Watties Tournament,
Poverty Bay Golf Club,
Gisborne.
NEW ZEALAND.

16th December, 1969.

Mr. G. Naismith,
128 Male Street,
North Brighton,
Victoria, 3186,
AUSTRALIA.

Dear Mr. & Mrs. Naismith,

    Just a short note to let you know some of the current news. During my last visit to Melbourne for the Dunlop International I met a gentleman by the name of Mr. Bucky Woy, who has signed me up for a contract which is including the American Circuit. As you can well imagine I am very pleased with this new deal, and I hope that during our association I can do justice to the amount of money in which he is investing in me. He also will be sponsoring me to the Far East, England and the Continent and to make the arrangement even better he has guaranteed the expenses for my wife also. Later in the year I will be going to America to try and get a players card so you can see that the progress in which I have made over the last couple of years has now proved successful. I feel that you have helped me tremendously and I am writing to you to let you know the good news. I must also apologise for not ringing you during my last visit to Melbourne, but you know how it is when you are travelling. I trust that Mrs. Naismith is in the best of health and that you are catching plenty of fish.

    I took a quick trip to Riversdale on my last visit and was very disappointed as I feel that the professional shop out there seems to have gone if any backwards since we left. It is certainly not like the old team used to be.

    The New Zealand circuit is going smoothly although I am not winning a great deal of money this is probably owing to the fact that I have been worrying about confirmation of my new contract, now that it has been confirmed I hope that I can now settle down again and play some good golf. I am looking forward very much to next year as it will be involving a great deal of golf and a lot of travelling so I hope that what I have learnt over the last few years eventually does stand by me. I will be coming down for the Victorian Open which I believe is in late February or early March and would very sincerely this time like either to come and see you and if possible we may be able to go and have dinner so I can explain to you more fully my new arrangements. So until then I wish you both well and look forward to seeing you very shortly. I would also like to take this opportunity of wishing you and your wife a very merry Christmas and a prosperous new year for 1970.

Yours faithfully,

David Graham.

April 1, 1970

Mr. and Mrs. George Naismith
128 Male Street
North Brighton
Victoria, Australia 3816

Dear Mr. and Mrs. Naismith:

Just a short note to let you know a little bit about my travel and golf at present. You have possibly read in the newspapers about my very fortunate success in Tasmania and Victoria and New South Wales. I was also fortunate to win last week the Thailand Open.

Maureen and I were in Victoria and, on two occasions, tried to ring you at home but there was no answer. We did want very much to see you during the Victoria Open and I had hoped that you may have come to Riversdale but I am sure even if time had allowed you to come to the tournament, you possibly would have given it second thoughts because it was held at Riversdale. The victory at Riversdale gave me a great deal of pleasure and I only wished you had been there to share it with me.

I saw and met many of the members who were there back in the good old days. It was quite funny to me because at first they didn't really care whether they spoke to me or not but on Sunday night, I found that I had more friends than I knew what to do with. I guess I'm tarred with the same brush as you. I am referring to the fact that my memory is not that short.

Digressing a little from that point of view, it was, however, a great thrill for my wife and I did win regardless of what course it was played on. The Asian tour this year is much busier and more competitive and the most pleasant thing about the victory in Bangkok was that I received an invitation to play in a $200,000. tournament in London.

After the Asian tour, I have plans to try my luck in qualifying for the U. S. Open. From there I hope to go to the British Open before coming back home to play our major tournaments. From there I will be going to America to try and get my players ticket at the PGA school which is held in November.

Appendix I

EMERALD HILLS COUNTRY CLUB

4100 NORTH HILLS DRIVE
HOLLYWOOD, FLORIDA 33021
TELEPHONE 961-4000

November 14, 1972

Mr. George Narsmith
12 Male St.
Brighton, Victoria
Australia

Dear Mr. and Mrs. Narsmith:

I am writing to you to offer my sincere apologies for not visiting you during my visit to Melbourne. It seems that each year I return home, I have less time to see my most personal friends. My wife and I called in to MSD to see you but, unfortunately, you were at home. The gentleman I spoke to informed me that in recent months your health has not been 100%. I feel what you need is a little more fishing and definitely, I prescribe more duck shooting. To heck with the pills. Just go catch some more fish.

I hope in the last twelve months you have followed my progress. I cannot help but think back several years to the day you spent with me at Riversdale when I was playing left-handed. I am sure happy now I have proven to everyone concerned how much you have contributed to my success. Just the advice alone to play right handed would have been enough, but during our association I learned many more valuable assets and I cannot put into words my appreciation.

I wish you and your wife continued happiness and the very best of health.

Best wishes,

David Graham

DG:aw
David Graham

David A. Graham

3901 N. 36TH AVENUE, HOLLYWOOD, FLORIDA 33021

November 19, 1974

Mr. and Mrs. George Naismith
12 Male Street
Brighton, Victoria, Australia

Dear Mr. and Mrs. Naismith:

    Just a brief letter to let you know I am now a father - in fact, a very proud father of a 5 lb. 8-1/2 ozs. baby boy. Both mother and child are doing just find. I have had my anniversary, birthday and Christmas present all at once.

    I am sorry we did not get a chance to meet during my visit but that is no reflection on the way that I have and will continue to feel about our relationship. The older I get, the more aware I become of what you did for me in what I call, the good old days. I will be home again next year, so let's definitely make a dinner date right now.

    Kindest regards,

                                Sincerely yours,

                                David Graham

DAG:med

david graham

November 26, 1975

Mr. George Naismith
12 Male Street
Brighton, Victoria
AUSTRALIA

Dear Mr. and Mrs. Naismith:

We all arrived home safely in Florida after an extremely tiring trip.

I just want to drop you a short note to let you know how much I enjoyed seeing you again this year. I only hope that one of these years when I return home that we can get together. We say this every year, but it never happens. For this reason, we should here and now commit ourselves to do it in 1976.

I cannot express enough appreciation for the way in which I felt having you walk with me during the final 18 at the Wills. I am sure that it meant alot towards making my victory possible. The only other thing that I can do is to reiterate the comments that I made during the presentation. I can assure you that I meant every word of it.

One of these days, you are going to have to come over to the U. S. to visit with us. I am sure you would have a most enjoyable time.

I look forward to hearing from you sometime in the near future.

Best wishes,

David Graham

David Graham

ca

david graham

August 10, 1976

Mr. George Nalsmith
128 Male Street
North Brighton 3186
Victoria
Australia

Thank you for your most welcome letter. It is happening isn't it? Just as you predicted. Thirty years old and just starting to make the big dollars. Can you recall what I said at the presentation during the Wills tournament? I think it would be very appropriate of me to reiterate what I said during that presentation.

I will be returning home to play in three tournaments, but specifically to concentrate on the Australian Open in Sydney. I would very much like for you and your wife to be my guests in Sydney during that week.

I hope all is going well for you and I do look forward to seeing you when I return home.

Very best wishes,

David

David Graham

ca

Appendix I

GOLF & TENNIS CLUB, INC.

625 GREENSWARD LANE/DELRAY BEACH, FLORIDA 33445/TELEPHONE 305.276-0351 (BROWARD 428-9130) (MIAMI 944-0791)

DAVID GRAHAM

August 24, 1979

Mr. George Naismith
128 Male Street
North Brighton 3186
Victoria, Australia

Dear George;

Well, what can I say?

I finally did it, and I am still having trouble getting over the excitement. I have played a lot of golf in the last few years and never have I experienced anything so exhausting, exciting and enjoyable as what I went through at the PGA.

I realize a great deal of press has been written - some good, some bad. I will never be able to repay the debt that I owe you. I would like for you to know just how grateful I really am.

I am bringing my whole family home this year and will be spending two weeks in Melbourne and I look forward to seeing you and Mary at that time.

Yours sincerely,

David Graham
DG:CDN

127

APPENDIX II

He's a handsome man of 27, short, well-groomed hair, slender build, and dressed impeccably. Somehow we tend to size up a golfer by his earnings, so I'll mention he won $57,827 last year and $67,889 in his career. The purses outside the United States were peanuts.

That's why he decided to take up residence at Hollywood's Emerald Hills Country Club and play the PGA tour. But this week it's Tournament Golf International (TGI) and Bardmoor Country Club. He arrived yesterday afternoon and didn't get around to hitting his first ball on the North Course until 3:15 p.m.

He wanted to talk some more, but had to get some practice and see as much of the North Course as possible before dark. Somewhere in between talking about the gas situation and knocking his first shot some 275 yards down the first fairway, there was a moment of silence.

The question was innocent enough. It's almost standard.

"Are you married?"

"Yes," he replied.

"Any children?"

That's when his head bowed and he toyed with the putter he had carried to the first tee.

"We had two," he finally said after a pause, searching for the right words.

DAVID GRAHAM

Why did I ask? I asked myself. It was my turn to hesitate and meditate.

"Was it an accident?" I finally asked.

"My wife gave birth to premature twins a couple months ago," he said in a somber voice, showing it still bothered him. "One boy was three days old and the other was five."

"I'm sorry, I didn't know," I said. "I'm surprised I didn't see anything about it on the wires."

"I didn't release it," he said. "It's not known."

Still somber, but not in a meditating way, he told of the 18-hole golf exhibition he is going to conduct at Emerald Hills in March with Jack Nicklaus, Bruce Devlin and himself.

"Proceeds from the exhibition will go to the hospital where my babies were born," Graham said. "They will go to the Memorial Hospital for treatment of premature and newly borns. Maybe (the money) will give them a little room to work with in the treatment of premature babies. It might be just enough to pay one pediatrian a year, but it's something.

"We're hoping to open the fourth spot for bids to anyone in the country. One chap not long ago paid $40,000 to play with Arnold Palmer in the National Airlines Pro-Am. I don't expect that much this time, but Nicklaus is the hottest player going right now. I'm sure a lot of guys would like to play with him."

Maybe so David, but somehow I get the feeling a lot of people would feel honored playing a round with you, too.

Excerpt from The Evening Independent *(Florida) of 7 December 1973. Sports news editor, Bill Robinson, reveals a previously unknown and tragic event in the lives of David and Maureen Graham.*

APPENDIX III

SYDNEY MORNING HERALD
Thursday 1 August 1996

I'M GUILTY OF NOTHING, RETORTS PUZZLED GRAHAM
Peter Stone

A deeply hurt David Graham has all but decided against taking legal action over his forced resignation as captain of the International team to play the US in the President's Cup next month, but he will wear the scars of the political battle forever. Graham, former US Open and US PGA champion, met his lawyer in Dallas, Texas, on Tuesday to discuss possible action for damages against the international players who brought about his downfall.

Two meetings of the international players were held during the British Open. Graham's captaincy was questioned and a joint statement was issued by the South African and Australasian PGA Tours announcing his resignation.

Five-time British Open champion Peter Thomson has since been named as his replacement for the second of the biennial President's Cup teams' series, to be played from September 12-15 at Lake Manassas in Virginia.

"I don't understand it. I am guilty of nothing. There is nothing they should disrespect me for," Graham said yesterday. "Out of all this, my name has been tarnished, my credibility has been tarnished.

"I believe the character of some of the (International) team members has been brought into question by the events of these past few weeks."

Among those in line for selection in the International team, which will be taken strictly from the world rankings as they stand in 10 days, are Greg Norman, Ernie Els, Nick Price, Steve Elkington, Michael Campbell, Frank Nobilo, Vijay Singh, Craig Parry, Robert Allenby and Peter Senior.

Graham claims he refused to tender his resignation as captain to either Brian Allan (chief executive of the Australasian Tour) or Brent Chalmers (of the South African Tour), but, when the mood of some players was made apparent to him, he resigned to USPGA Tour executive director Tim Finchem. At the same time, he resigned his membership of the Australasian Tour.

"I have cancelled my Australasian PGA membership, but I am still a member in good standing with the USPGA," said Graham, who, last month began life on the US Seniors' circuit. At the weekend, he tied fourth in the Ameritech Open at Kemper Lakes, in Illinois, collecting $75,000.

Graham says he is surprised that Thomson has accepted the role of captain.

"Peter Thomson is an excellent choice, but not under these circumstances," Graham said. "By accepting, he is condoning the actions of the players who, he says, have acted irresponsibly.

"I spoke with Peter recently and he told me he felt he should step in to salvage whatever there is to salvage from the series.

"I just wish he had given it more thought."

The alleged charge against Graham was a lack of communication and planning for the President's Cup with the prospective players. They claimed not to have heard from him, but he denies this, saying they have been forwarded all relevant information.

It is the custom in the biennial Ryder Cup match between the US and Europe for the captain of each team to present each of his players, and their wives, with a small gift, and Graham followed that ritual last time around in the President's Cup two years ago.

He intended to do the same thing again next month.

"My wife (Maureen) went to New York and bought a number of gifts. They have all been personalised for the players and their wives. What do I do with them now?" he asked.

There is no doubting the whole sorry episode has been badly mishandled, but Graham's hope is that it will not endanger the future of the President's Cup, which was a teams series created only after some serious lobbying of the USPGA.

INDEX

A

Air New Zealand Open 71
Allis, Peter v, vi, 51, 52
American Golf Classic 48, 59
Aoki, Isao 116
Appleby, Stuart 79
Australian Golf Club, The (Australia) 20, 53, 56
Australian Open Championship 13, 14, 19, 20, 35, 36, 40, 41, 43, 49, 53, 55-58, 62, 69, 83, 86, 90, 91, 96
Australian PGA Championship 27, 36
Australian Masters 90

B

Baker-Finch, Ian 23, 53, 102
Ballesteros, Severiano 71, 72
Bank of America Championship 109
Barrot, Bill 17
Bembridge Maurice 40
Bodney, Mike 103
Brewer, Gay 39
British Open 40, 42, 53, 65, 68, 83, 88, 101, 103, 115, 116, 129
Brown, John 107
Burns, George 74-76

C

Cabrera, Angel 67
Cairns Open 26
Campbell, Chad 67
Caracas Open 37
Chrysler Classic Tournament 39, 91
Chunichi Crowns Tournament 47
Clayton, Michael 30, 101
Cleveland Open 38
Colonial Country Club (USA) 38, 43
Couples, Fred 60, 106
Crampton, Bruce 33, 62

Crandon Park Golf Club (USA) 94
Crean, John 8
Cremin, Eric 22, 23
Crenshaw, Ben 60, 62, 65, 66, 68, 74

D

Davies, Judy Joy 19
de Groot, Colin 24
de Vicenzo, Roberto 33
Devlin, Bruce vi, 27, 28, 33, 34, 38, 43, 52, 54, 75, 103-105, 113-116
Dillon, Jack 78
Doan, Joe 60
Dunhill Cup 34-37, 101, 115
Dunk, Bill 27, 29, 92
Dunlop International 28

E

Elder, Lee 86
Elkington, Steve 102, 104, 107, 115, 129
Els, Ernie 101, 102, 129

F

Faldo, Nick 47
Feherty, David 37
Finchem, Tim 103, 104, 116, 130
Firestone Country Club (USA) 48
Floyd, Raymond 51, 54, 79
Forbes Golf Club (Australia) 25
French Open 32

G

Gitsham, Lindsay 17
Golf Hall of Fame 116
Graham, George 9, 10
Graham, Maureen (nee Burdett) 10, 26, 28, 32, 40, 45, 49, 67, 75, 76, 81, 112, 114, 128, 130
Graham (Waisito), Patricia 5, 7, 8, 10, 11, 19, 20, 88
Green, Hubert 54
Greenbrier Classic 79
Greensboro Open 53

H

Hagen, Walter 75
Hartley, Kevin 30
Hazeltine Golf Club (USA) 10
Heublin Classic 72
Higson, Claire 22
Hinkle, Lon 73
Hogan, Ben vi, 61, 75, 76
Hong Kong Open 28
Hudson, Neil 7
Huntingdale Golf Club (Australia) 90

I

Ingham, John 62
International Golf Association 33
Iron Horse Golf Club (USA) 110, 111
Irwin, Hale 51, 73, 99

J

Jacklin, Tony 78
January, Don 54, 55
Japan Airlines Open 37
Jockey Club (Argentina) 33

K

Kingston Heath Golf Club (Aust) 9, 17
Kooyonga Golf Club (Aust) 40

L

Lakes Golf Club, The (Australia) 39, 69
Lancome Trophy 81, 86
Langer, Bernhard 88, 90
Lyle, Sandy 88, 90, 116

M

McBee, Rives 111
McCleary, Jonathan 107
McDonnell, Michael 67
McIlroy, Rory 36
Marsh, Graham 34-36, 86
Masters Cup and Tee Committee 97
Mercer, Alex 26
Merion Golf Club (USA) 22, 32, 73-82, 89, 110
Metropolitan Golf Club (Australia) 27
Mexico Cup 58, 59
Mickelson, Phil 36, 116
Miller, Johnny 83
Moody, Orville 28, 29
Moonah Links Golf Club (Australia) 96
Morfit, Cameron 47, 106
Murphy, Bob 94

N

Naismith, George 8, 9, 13-20, 22, 29, 30, 40, 46, 54, 56, 57, 78, 86-88, 91, 107, 114, 117
New South Wales Open 30
Newport Beach Golf Club (USA) 94
Newton, Jack 35, 39, 72
Nicklaus, Jack vi, 23, 27, 32, 34, 36, 43-45, 47, 53-56, 58, 59, 61, 68, 71, 74, 83
Nobilo, Frank 102, 103, 129
Norman, Greg 34, 36, 37, 42, 83, 100-104, 106, 107, 115, 116, 118, 129

O

Oakland Hills Golf Club (USA) 32, 59-61, 63, 64, 66, 67, 74
Oatlands Golf Club (Australia) 73
Olympic Golf Club (USA) 111
O'Meara, Mark 91

P

Palmer, Arnold 27, 28, 32, 36, 47, 100, 111
Panks, Gary 95
Parry, Craig 60, 129
Pate, Jerry 54, 73
Patey, Bob 7
Pebble Beach Golf Club (USA) 58, 75
Perry, Kenny 66, 67
Peterson, Willie 61, 62, 67
Phillips, Frank 30, 31
Phoenix Open 73
Player, Gary 23, 27, 36, 46, 47, 52, 59, 74, 101, 105
Precision Golf Forgings 22, 23, 25, 28, 52
Prendergast Paul, 116
Presidents Cup 94, 99-107, 115
Preston Trail Golf Club (USA) 93
Pymble Golf Club (Australia) 24

Q

Queensland Open 35, 92
Queensland PGA Championship 27

R

Riversdale Golf Club (Australia) v, 8, 9, 13, 15-18, 20, 22, 30, 31, 52, 54, 88, 107, 117
Robert Trent Jones Golf Club (USA) 99
Rogers, Bill 74, 83
Ross, Donald 60
Royal Birkdale Golf Club (England) 53
Royal Caribbean Classic 94
Royal Lytham and St Annes Golf Club (England) 103
Royal Melbourne Golf Club (Australia) 91, 106
Royal St George's Golf Club (England) 88
Ryder Cup 99, 104, 105, 130

S

St Andrews Golf Club (Scotland) 34
Seabrook Golf Club (Australia) 22, 23, 25
Shearer, Bob 35, 36
Shinnecock Hills Golf Club (USA) 79
Sigel, Jay 94
Singapore Open 28
Singh, Vijay 47, 106, 129
Smith, Terry 38, 40, 52
Snead, Sam 32
South African PGA Championship 53
Stacy, Hollis 116
Stanley, Ian 91, 92
Stephenson, Jan 72
Stockton, Dave 94
Stone, Peter 104, 129

T

Taiheyo Masters 39
Tasmanian Open 29
Thailand Open 31
Thomson, Peter 13, 27, 30, 40-42, 56, 62, 86, 91, 96, 100, 102, 103, 107, 115, 116, 118, 129, 130
Thorpe, Jim 86
Toshiba Classic 94
Trevino, Lee 28, 29, 34, 48, 75, 76, 86, 104, 111, 113, 114
Turtle Point Golf Club (Australia) 96

U

US Masters 32, 37, 52, 60, 66-68, 71, 73, 87, 90, 97, 107, 111
US Open Championship 109, 111, 114, 115, 129
US PGA Championship 115, 129

V

Van de Veld, Jean 68
Victoria Golf Club (Australia) 40, 46, 83
Victorian Boys Championship 18
Victorian Open 30, 31
Von Nida, Norman 13, 26

W

Ward-Thomas, Pat 41
Watson, Tom 58
Wattle Park Golf Club (Australia) 6-8, 16
Webb, Karrie 116
Webster, Jim 113
Weiskopf, Tom 71, 72, 76, 113
Wentworth Golf Club (England) 47, 49
Westchester Classic 48
West Lakes Classic 71, 72
Williams, Frank 101, 102
Wills Masters 46
Wind, Herbert Warren 75
Woodlands Golf Club (Australia) 17
Woods, Ernie 9
Woods, Tiger 36, 47
Woosnam, Ian 34
World Cup 33, 34, 115
World Match Play Championship 36, 47, 48, 51, 53
World Mixed Teams Championship 72
Woy, Bucky 29, 31, 39, 47, 48
Wright, Alfred 61

Y

Yarra Yarra Golf Club (Australia) 28
Yomiuri International 31, 47

www.ingramcontent.com/pod-product-compliance
Lightning Source LLC
Chambersburg PA
CBHW070734230426
43665CB00016B/2231